T0329470

POLITICAL PHILOSOPHY

POLITICAL PHILOSOPHY

THE NARROW PATH OF SOCIAL PROGRESS

ANTHONY C. PATTON

Algora Publishing
New York

Library of Congress Cataloging-in-Publication Data —

Names: Patton, Anthony C., 1969- author.
Title: Political philosophy: the narrow path of social progress / Anthony C.
    Patton.
Description: New York: Algora Publishing, 2017. | Includes bibliographical
    references.
Identifiers: LCCN 2017015062 (print) | LCCN 2017016561 (ebook) | ISBN
    9781628942873 (pdf) | ISBN 9781628942859 (soft cover: alk. paper) | ISBN
    9781628942866 (hard cover: alk. paper)
Subjects: LCSH: Universals (Philosophy) | Teleology.
Classification: LCC B105.U5 (ebook) | LCC B105.U5 P38 2017 (print) | DDC
    110—dc23
LC record available at https://lccn.loc.gov/2017015062

Printed in the United States

TABLE OF CONTENTS

> Moral communities are fragile things, hard to build and
> easy to destroy. When we think about very large commu-
> nities such as nations, the challenge is extraordinary and
> the threat of moral entropy is intense. —Jonathan Haidt

The search for what this book is about begins with my previous
book, *The Political Spectrum: The Rational Foundations of Liberty and
Prosperity*. My hope is this book stands alone as a positive contribution
to the debate, but just as I could not have written this book without
having first written *The Political Spectrum*, the reader of this book
would benefit from first reading *The Political Spectrum*. I will highlight
and summarize key points from that book to advance the argument
in this book, but this will not be sufficient to convey what the reader
needs to know and understand.

The primary goal of *The Political Spectrum* was to analyze two of the
most important outside-the-mind truths about society (in particular, a
modern state) that will help us shape the political debate in important
ways. The first outside-the-mind truth, in the context of resource
management, was that society as a whole must be a net producer of
resources to sustain society. To show why this is true, if we think
about society as a water bucket with a slow leak, then to prevent the
bucket from going empty, we have to add enough water to the bucket
to offset the loss of water from the leak, or we will find ourselves with
an empty bucket. This is a mathematical fact that should shape our
behavior. This truth is important for political philosophy because it
means that resource production should take primacy over resource
distribution. Focusing our attention on resource production might
make our resource distribution system seem less than fair or just

at times, depending on your definition of fair or just, but the only thing worse than this would be focusing our attention on resource distribution at the expense of resource production, which would result in an empty bucket, which would not be fair to anyone. Just as we cannot reap unless we sow, we cannot distribute the goods of society unless we first establish a way to produce them.

The second outside-the-mind truth about society was that men and women must unite in an institution of procreation and have an average of at least two children per couple to sustain the population, or more if the goal is to grow society. This is also a mathematical fact that should shape our behavior. If China were to continue its one child policy, the population of China would steadily decline over time, with each generation half as large as the previous generation. When we consider how long it takes for children to reach biological maturity and how much children depend on altruistic love, which necessarily entails personal sacrifice from the parents who are responsible for raising them, I concluded that the best way to sustain society was to promote the sanctity of monogamous procreation. This way, children would be raised by the people nature by design inspires to make the necessary sacrifices for them and to actually find satisfaction in the sacrifice. People on a bell curve distribution will never make the necessary sacrifices for strangers. Some people might be willing to make these sacrifices, but not the population as whole, at least not in a way that would make for responsible public policy. This way, we can set a standard of expecting adults to sacrifice their own hopes and dreams, to a reasonable degree, to ensure all children receive the attention and love they need to become mature adults who pay it forward to their own children. If we fail to do this, if we fail to produce the next generation and fail to make the necessary sacrifices for our children by paying it forward, social entropy will result.

After finishing *The Political Spectrum*, I continued to ruminate on the ideas of political philosophy and concluded the well was not dry and there were more ideas to explore—new perspectives and new depths. In particular, I realized that the society I presumed in *The Political Spectrum* was a functional modern state, and my analysis was focused on how to sustain a modern state, like a mature adult writing about how to be a mature adult. What was missing from my analysis was lifting the veil of society to understand the dynamic process of making the transition from subsistence farming to a modern state, to make the transition from innocent childhood to functional adulthood, what I will refer to in this book as the narrow path. For example, as societies grow in size and complexity, and hunting and gathering no longer suffice to feed the population, it becomes necessary to invent the technology of agriculture and livestock to avoid starvation. Depending on geography, climate, soil, and the local flora and fauna, some ways of farming and raising livestock are better than others. We can calculate how many acres we should plant and harvest to feed the population, given a particular yield. We can calculate how many animals or pounds of meat we need to feed the population, and so on, with the understanding that the transition to agriculture and livestock changes the way we grow and develop as humans.

Some technology is developed by trial and error or tinkering, but with hindsight technology is not a fluke because it is grounded in reality—it works, like agriculture and livestock. Any society that fails to implement this technology to feed its population will grind to a halt on the narrow path of social progress. Populations must grow beyond a certain threshold to make the complexity of a modern state possible, and this growth requires food. We have to get each step right on the narrow path before we move on to the next challenge, but nature does not provide us a map and we should remember that the development of our human potential is a critical part of the narrow path. The same idea applies to other technologies, such as building shelter, establishing police and military institutions to protect us from threats, collecting and purifying water, creating money to facilitate the exchange of goods and services, and so on. Much of this technology requires the power of rational minds and must be sustained generation after generation. The technology will never magically take care of itself. Just as we must apply technology to the world we live in, we also must invent human technology to help society continue along the narrow path, such as learning mathematics and science, the virtues and delayed gratification, methods to promote cooperation among strangers, the science of diet, or arts and letters, and so on. Our minds are designed to think quantitatively, but rational minds must create a base-ten numbering system.

The take away is that we can imagine a narrow path of social progress that takes us from subsistence farming to fulfilling our potential within a modern state. Staying on the narrow path is challenging, for individuals and for society, but straying from the path is easy, as there are many suboptimal exit ramps along the way. And the longer we are off the narrow path, the harder it is to get back on, just as our aerobic capacity decreases if we stop exercising. The question I will address in this book is, what are the human and social technologies that keep us on the narrow path? The various academic disciplines can address the specifics of how agriculture and mathematics work, but to understand what all these ideas and technologies have in common across disciplines and what makes them possible, we have to turn to philosophy.

After reflecting on the narrow path in the context of the history of philosophy, I concluded that the analysis in many ways boils down to the problem of universals and the related idea of teleology. Just as DNA pervades the study of biology and the idea of numbers pervades the study of mathematics, the problem of universals and teleology pervade the study of political philosophy and the study of the narrow path of personal and social progress. Time and again I have read books about political philosophy that are loaded with assumptions about universals and teleology, even though these two words are usually never mentioned. In fact, many authors might not even be familiar with universals and teleology. Along these lines, I concluded that people with a particular view of universals and teleology tend to adhere to predictable principles of political philosophy, and people with a particular view of political philosophy tend to adhere to predictable principles of universals and teleology. The two sides go hand in hand, and this analysis will help us understand why liberals and conservatives are so often unable to see eye to eye. They make different assumptions about key issues. What many people consider cohesive or consistent ideas about political philosophy are natural extensions of more fundamental beliefs regarding universals and teleology.

In the case of universals, the big question is whether there is anything stable or eternal behind the flux of appearance and perceptions, outside the mind, that can serve as a foundation or stepping stone for truth to keep us on the narrow path, personally and socially. If I say "agriculture," is this idea grounded in reality, independent of human thought (soil, water, sunlight, nutrients, seeds, weather, etc.), or is it merely a convenient way to group together certain types of activities for our own convenience, in which case it might be subject to change in the future? To think about the question another way, when we consider solving a technical problem, like landing a man on the moon, do we think the solution will be found through chance and will work one time, or do we believe there is an eternal mathematical formula "out there" waiting to be discovered that we know with certainty will vector our spacecraft safely to the surface of the moon, now and forever? Or, when we train for the Olympics, do we go with our gut or do we believe there is an objective way to nourish and train our body for optimal performance?

In the case of teleology, from the day we are born, the human body is in a constant state of growth and decay, and yet we can talk about the essence of a human being or of humans striving for things that are consistent with their nature. Looking through the lens of teleology means accepting that our standards for behavior should be grounded in our organism and our nature, and that not all ways of thinking and behaving should be treated with equal respect. Some diets are better than others; some ways of exercising are better than others; some ways of educating ourselves are better than others; some ways of thinking about political philosophy are better than others; some virtues are more worthy of being developed than others, and so on. When our analysis combines a valid understanding of universals and teleology, we set the stage for walking the narrow path of social progress.

The idea of the narrow path of personal and social progress makes sense only if we measure it against an objective standard because the idea of progress suggests motion toward something qualitatively better, such as the transition from subsistence farming to a modern state. Otherwise, we would have to refer to personal or social progress as personal or social change, with no qualitative assessment of one system being better than another. There might not be universal agreement on the objective standard, but history has given us strong indications that people around the world seem to strive for something resembling modern state democracy, with a right to participate in the political process and to hold political leaders accountable. Despite this widely accepted observation, some people might take issue with modern state democracy, for two reasons.

First, some might argue that too much democracy is not always good and that if history has taught us anything, it is that popular vote is not always the best way to make important decisions. Just as a military commander would never allow the troops to vote on the direction of the battle, there are some decisions that governments should make without consulting the voters. This argument has merits and deserves our attention, but it is not a fundamental criticism because it still supports the basic idea of modern state democracy. Second, some might argue that there is no objective standard of social progress, that one system is not better than another. In other words, truth is relative and changes from time to time, from place to place, and from person to person. This argument is a fundamental criticism of the idea of social progress because it reduces social activity to directionless motion. Proponents of this view might suggests that having food is better than starving or that non-violence is better than violence—in other words, people as a matter of fact strive for some things and avoid other things—but they would have us believe all of our judgments are subject to change in the future when the circumstances change. They would have us believe there is no such thing as truth.

Finally, as I have learned over the years, writing a book does not happen in a vacuum. I am responsible for overall direction of the book and take full responsibility for any and all flaws and errors, but I also recognize that no man is an island and this book would not be possible without the people in my life. First, I would like to thank my lovely wife Doranellys and our three wonderful sons, who with patience and understanding encouraged me to grind away one page at a time, usually on nights and weekends. They understand my passion for philosophy and helped me every step of the way. You will never know how much your love means to me. Second, I would like to thank Andrea, Martin, and the team at Algora Publishing for pushing me to write the best books possible and for helping my ideas see the light of day. Political philosophy is contentious by nature and rooted in our brainstems, so it requires the diligent yet delicate hands of editors to keep the train of thought from going off the rails. The writer's journey is often solitary and frustrating, but confidence builds and ideas flow more smoothly when a book finds a home.

PART I. THE TELESCOPE

CHAPTER ONE. AS ABOVE

The question is often asked—what separates humans from other animals? A widely accepted answer, one I happen to agree with, is our capacity for reason, concepts, and language, which in turn provides us a capacity for art, imagination, and new insights about life. Unlike other animals that live in the present, humans have the ability to pause the journey of life, take stock of what is happening—past, present, and future—and chart a course on the narrow path before we continue the journey. From the time we are born, our minds automatically begin to conceptualize, and as we go through life we develop a web or hierarchy of concepts that grows and gets pruned, we hope, in a way that reflects reality and allows us to live as mature human beings.

If done correctly, this web or hierarchy of concepts will allow us to fill in some of the gaps of our perceptual blind spots and to make practical decisions or gain insights about the world and how to live. However, to the extent that reason allows us to rise above nature, the improper use of reason allows us to sink below nature, often in horrifying ways, taking the horrors of WWI and WWII as examples. Just as a machete can be used to cut open the top of a chilled coconut to enjoy the tasty liquid on a sweltering hot day, the same machete can be used to cut open the skull of an enemy tribe member. As we use our power of reason to make sense of the world and walk the narrow path of personal and social progress, rather than wandering aimlessly, we are working with universals.

If we want to build a project in the real world, such as a bridge or a building, we have to gather the right materials, the right equipment and tools, and the right workers to move the project along. In addition to this, however, we also have to get the ideas right—the intangible ideas that hold the project together. For example, if we want to build a bridge, we have to use the right materials in the right way to make sure the bridge can withstand heavy vehicles and strong winds. We could take the path of the beaver and pile up sticks until we achieve a desired result, which might work for a small footbridge over a creek, but we have to do better if we want to build four-lane bridges that span canyons or connect islands. We need engineering.

Taking the example of a building, not only do we have to consider the same issues in terms of the structure of the building, we also have to consider the people who will occupy the building, such as how much space each person needs to be productive, how many bathrooms, how many emergency exits, lighting, temperature, electrical outlets, and the list goes on. Everyone has had the experience of seeing a building or a house that "doesn't work." By this we mean it doesn't work for humans. Another species or an alien race might find it perfectly suitable. These intangible ideas and formulas that we use to complete these projects are universals. They are the steppingstones amidst the flux that make knowledge, progress, and modern states possible.

In many ways, developing a political philosophy is like developing the plan for a bridge or building. However, rather than use universals to select the materials to build things, we use universals to provide a philosophical structure (ideas and ideas about ideas) to our lives with the understanding that we are biological organisms with a particular nature who are living in a world that appears to be uniform, not random. Political philosophy and human life would not work in a world of Brownian motion or quantum randomness. For example, it would not be wise to structure our educational system to end at the age of 6 or 60 if we know that humans develop and mature in such a way that ending our formal education during our late teens or early twenties is a better fit. This age allows for continued education during our career and allows for enough productive working years to keep society chugging along in an optimal way. We cannot perceive this truth in the same way we perceive colors or sounds, but we can build a web or hierarchy of universals that allow us to make wise decisions about these practical matters.

Likewise, once we understand our basic needs like food, shelter, and love, we can structure how we live in the world to ensure that we produce enough food (the science of livestock and agriculture) and have living arrangements that take into consideration our need to bond and have a shared community experience. Having each person live alone to manage a plot of land in isolation, even if the material results were good, would be unfulfilling and would result in failure. At a minimum, men and women would have to be paired up to continue the species, but they would probably find themselves joining other families to form a community. We could rely on hunting and gathering if we are willing to live in bands or small tribes, with the hope of finding enough food and avoiding enemy attack, but once we decide to grow our populations and social complexity toward a modern state, we have to introduce the universals of food science to ensure we satisfy our dietary requirements, which is impossible without universals.

Humans rely on universals because we are unique in the animal kingdom. All other species are born ready to survive for the most part and adapt themselves to the environment they live in. There are no potential Aristotles, Newtons, or Mozarts in the animal kingdom. Granted, many other animals learn by imitation and take steps to manipulate the environment to suit their own needs, such as building shelters or dams, but nothing on the level we see with humans. More important, all other animals living in nature for the most part achieve their organic maturity as a matter of course. The animal kingdom is not filled with social outcasts or revolutionary groups. If we find a lion hunting in the plains of Africa, we are observing a creature living in accordance with its full potential. It is not the case that lions would build a modern state and write poetry if given the chance, but for the fact that they are stuck living in the plains of Africa without sufficient resources for education. In a state of nature, lions are living in accordance with their nature—hunting, eating, sleeping, and mating.

In the case of humans, the game is different. In a so-called "state of nature," humans are incapable of living in accordance with their full potential. Something resembling education and leisure are required before we see the likes of Shakespeare. One of the goals of this book is to address this difficult "chicken or egg" conundrum (the narrow path) in which people who are not living in accordance with their full potential find ways to transcend the limitations of their current circumstances, by design or by luck, to move closer to fulfilling their potential. As most people have come to accept, people who are raised in squalor, crime, and abuse often cannot be expected to behave in accordance with the guidelines of refined civilization. Thus, one of the ideas I hope to convey in this book is that those of us who have the good fortune of living in developed countries are rightly said to be living in a state of nature, which has important implications for political philosophy. What follows from this is the idea that humans have a particular nature, but only potentially. Most people accept this intuitively, such as when we imagine our child qualifying for the Olympics after ten years of rigorous training. The child cannot do it today, but the theoretical potential exists.

We can therefore think about political philosophy in two ways. First, we have to reach a general consensus about what it means for humans to reach their potential. If we are going to establish pathways for people to reach their potential, which is beneficial for individuals and society, we have to know the possible paths and possible destinations. Is our nature fixed, are we blank slates, or are we somewhere between? Are all people the same or are there real differences that make us lean toward different paths or destinations, regardless of our environment? Some of these questions are empirical and can be answered by the social sciences, but others require philosophy. In many ways, this is the easy part of political philosophy: mapping out what people need to do as a matter of fact to achieve their potential.

Second, we have to understand what is required from each of us individually to sustain this complex system called a modern state, to avoid slipping into social entropy. That is, if a modern state has certain inputs and outputs that are required to sustain our existence at a certain level of size and complexity, then we should take steps to ensure that individuals contribute enough to keep the system sustainable. We all feed off and contribute to society in a variety of ways and in varying degrees, but this is empirical and can be quantified. If everyone takes a penny without ever giving a penny, we will eventually run out of pennies at the cash register. There is no doubt that we need altruistic assistance during our childhood and retirement, but we should never forget that real people are taking care of us during those years, often via taxes and personal effort. This is the more difficult part of political philosophy because it requires us to factor in not only the objective mathematics of life, such as raising taxes to fund social programs, but also to understand the people with complex motivations and incentives who will be asked to work longer hours or delay gratification to fund these programs.

THE SAME RIVER TWICE

Depending on the project, the universals we use should be reasonably unchanging and woven into the fabric of the world. For example, when building a bridge, we should rely on ideas like gravity and the strength of steel and concrete, which we can quantify with precision. The universe in theory perhaps could have been otherwise and we might one day discover stronger materials, but the possibility of science presumes the existence of universals or laws that are unchanging or woven into the fabric of the world. When Einstein postulated $E = mc^2$, he did not envision an annual update as the universe evolved; in fact, he envisioned this formula shaping the way the universe evolved. Often, the discovery of these universals is done within the realm of science, although intuition and philosophy are often important for leading us down the right path of discovering universals and gaining insights about the world. After all, some scientific theories are devised prior to the collection of evidence to confirm them, and some mathematical formulas are applied to reality with spectacular precision many years after their discovery.

Other situations are less rigid, such as human societies, because humans have a wide gap between potential and actual at any given moment of history. How we live will always be a function of the environment we live in and our stage of personal and social development. The laws of political philosophy are less rigid than the laws of nature. For example, the fact that Switzerland and Japan have achieved economic success with limited natural resources is proof that countries are not merely a product of their material environment. Whether an economy is dominated by agriculture, industry, or services, there seems to be a natural tendency of human societies over time toward a similar end point, what Fukuyama called "The End of History." They key point is we can talk about what "works" in a developing country, even though it is something we would not promote in a developed country. For example, we might tolerate limits on suffrage in a developing country if the average person is malnourished and uneducated, with the understanding that more people will be allowed to vote as the economy grows and more people are benefiting from diet and education.

This book focuses on political philosophy, not science, but we can use some scientific universals to shape our political philosophy. The major benefit of this is that it allows us to avoid the relativism that plagues many political philosophies. For example, some people might argue that because some of the universals of political philosophy are not eternal or woven into the fabric of world, truth is therefore relative. To wit, if one society makes decisions based on consulting a witch doctor and another society makes decisions based on consulting experts with reams of data, some would claim there is no objective way to judge the relative merits of the two systems. On the other hand, some societies have promoted or tolerated infanticide (Sparta) or pederasty (Athens), but most people living in modern states would reject them without regard for the circumstances or environment that gave rise to them.

According to those who espouse relativism, life is a matter of taste, nothing more, and we should not waste our time judging others about what is true for us or true for them. Although tolerance is an important part of political philosophy and living in a modern state, it does not follow that objective truth is impossible because people live differently as a matter of fact. In fact, the ideas of virtue and value make sense only if they have some objective foundation that does not depend on our opinion. Most people would agree that the answers to mathematical problems are true or false and are not relative just because two different people get two different answers. However, this discussion of relativism does give rise to an important point about universals that takes us back to the ancient Greece and the origins of philosophy.

Before Socrates, Plato, and Aristotle established the philosophical foundation for Western civilization, a group of philosophers known as the pre-Socratics tackled some important issues. The pre-Socratics are widely regarded as taking the first steps in making the transition from myth and superstition to philosophy and science. Rather than explain weather in terms of the behavior of angry gods, they looked for natural causes such as air pressure and moisture in the clouds. Although many of their ideas are best categorized as cosmological rather than philosophical, some of the ideas they raised, such as the "one and the many" or "permanence and change," still shape the debate today.

The pre-Socratics recognized that we find ourselves in a world of change and plurality but also recognized that there must exist some kind of permanence or oneness behind the change or plurality of nature if we are to make sense of it. That is, if we are going to understand the world and gain knowledge, there must be something unchanging that we understand, even if what we understand is the process of change; otherwise, by the next day it will change and we will have to get to know something else. What does it mean to say I know a person if the person today is not the same person he was yesterday or will be tomorrow? To know someone, we must know him as the same individual over time, and there must be something about me that remains throughout time that allows me to say I know him. The person will traverse the normal cycles of life but something of the original person persists along the way.

One philosopher, Heraclitus, took the extreme position that the world was in a constant state of flux, like fire, and that the idea of a permanence or oneness underlying the flux was an illusion. As Heraclitus said, "You never step in the same river twice." Somewhat implicit in this idea was that although the river always changes, the person stepping into the river has some sense of permanence that allows him to make the observation about change and permanence, which shows the challenge of being consistent about eternal change. Another philosopher, Parmenides, took the opposite extreme position that the world was one and permanent, with the world of change and plurality being an illusion. Although these two views might seem simplistic and easy to dismiss, they have shaped the philosophical debate through the ages, and many prominent thinkers since then have regressed to their errors, even in modern philosophy.

The first systematic attempt to resolve this problem was made by Plato, who was influenced by Heraclitus in terms of how he understood sense perception, by Parmenides in terms of how he understood ultimate reality, and by Pythagoras in terms of how he understood mathematics. Plato believed mathematics (numbers and geometric shapes) existed in a mysterious realm between sense perception and the ultimate, unchanging reality—the Forms or Ideas. Just as important, Plato relied on the method of Socrates to develop the definitions of important universals like Good and Justice. To avoid the scourge of relativism, the definitions for these universals should have a meaning that is not subject to the whims of people or the winds of change.

Plato, like Heraclitus, argued that sensory perception was in a constant state of flux and was therefore not a reliable foundation of knowledge. Our perceptions are not always reliable and often give us mixed signals. For example, cool water feels cold if our hands are hot but the same water feels warm if our hands are cold. (A thermometer, on the other hand, will give us the correct temperature each time.) Plato believed true knowledge must be of eternal and unchanging things, which takes us to universals. In the history of philosophy, Plato is considered a realist because he believed universals have an objective reality independent of human perception or cognition—outside the mind. For example, consider horses. Particular horses exist in the world, but to have true knowledge of horses, Plato said we had to go beyond the plurality of horses of perception to the single Horse in the nonmaterial realm of Forms or Ideas where the eternal universals exist. When we acquire knowledge of horses, we do so via the Forms or the Idea of Horse, which we achieve via the intellect, not via perception.

Plato also believed in the Form or Idea of abstract ideas like Good or Justice, which is important for political philosophy. The theory of Forms or Ideas raises difficult questions such as how we gain knowledge of the Forms or Ideas and how the objects of perception participate in or interact with these Forms and Ideas. However, many philosophers have argued that Plato's ideas merit our attention and that some of the confusion about Forms and Ideas stems from the difficulty of explaining them with human language and human understanding.

The second systematic attempt to resolve the problem universals was made by Aristotle, who focused on discrediting Plato's theory of Forms or Ideas and offering an interesting solution that provided a foundation for modern science. (For reasons that are not clear, many modern writers, especially in the social sciences, ignore or gloss over Aristotle.) Like Plato, Aristotle was a realist because he believed universals do not depend on human perception or cognition—outside the mind. Unlike Plato, however, Aristotle believed universals exist in the material world, not in an immaterial realm of Forms or Ideas. For example, in the case of horses, the essence of horse is embodied in the horse itself and is something all horses share. There is no need to posit the Form or Idea of Horse to account for the existence of particular horses. Thus, even though each horse is in a constant state of flux of growth and decay, from birth until death, we can gain knowledge about horses because there is something essential or eternal about these horses that makes knowledge of them possible, such as DNA.

With this analysis, Aristotle introduced the category of substance, which is beyond the scope of this book but had a lasting impact on the history of philosophy. Aristotle's answer to the problem of universals is widely considered an improvement on Plato, but just as important to our discussion is Aristotle's theory of actual versus potential. To avoid many of the problems about perpetual change that Heraclitus raised, Aristotle explained that, especially as it relates to biological organisms, things are in a constant process of actualizing a potential. For example, if we plant a peach seed, it will grow into a peach tree, not an apple tree or a lemon tree, no matter how much we manipulate the sunlight, water, soil, and nutrients. Implicit in any peach seed is a future peach tree, and the unfolding of this potential is what allows us to have knowledge of a particular tree, even if it is in a constant state of change.

Philosophers since Plato and Aristotle have continued to debate these issues. One of the most notable proposed solutions to the problem of universals was nominalism, which argued that universals are nothing more than thoughts in the minds of the people who think them. Taking justice as an example, what constitutes justice for one group of people might not constitute justice for another group of people, so the argument goes. However, if justice were a universal, we would all understand it the same way. Obviously, abstract concepts like justice are more difficult to define and apply to all people in all times and places, but this does not mean justice does not have a true meaning that manifests itself with greater clarity as people achieve biological growth and maturity and societies progress. For example, all reasonable people would agree that the murder of innocent people should be condemned in all times and all places. To the extent this is true, we can talk about justice in an objective way.

BEING, ETERNAL

Now that we have discussed the theory of universals, we can raise specific cases to gain a better understanding of universals. To begin with an example, consider gold. If we dismiss for now the Platonic Form or Idea of Gold as something existing in a nonmaterial realm and focus our attention on the gold of the world we live in, in mines or jewelry, we see gold has properties or predicates. We can describe the color, texture, taste, smell, and even the sound of gold if it is struck like a tuning fork, that is, everything that results from gold affecting our senses. To use the language of Locke, we can think of these properties or predicates as secondary qualities of gold because they depend on our senses but are grounded in the object. Something exists in the gold that gives rise to the qualia of our perceptions (sights, sounds, smells, and so on), but we cannot say with certainty whether these same properties or predicates inhere per se in the gold. Most important, although it should surprise no one that substances like gold are thought of as universals, so are the predicates that we apply to substances, such as colors, smells, tastes, textures, and so on. Gold the color and gold the substance are both universals. On the other hand, we can consider what Locke called primary qualities, such as solidity and extension, which are generally thought of as inhering in the gold whether or not people are there to perceive it. The most important difference between primary and secondary qualities is the fact that secondary qualities are unique to each sense organ whereas primary qualities can be perceived by more than one sense organ. For example, we can both see and touch the length of an object.

We can agree that gold has certain properties or predicates when we perceive it but this does not mean gold can be reduced to these same properties or predicates, evidenced by the fact that fool's gold has been known to make fools of us. Thus, if we want to arrive at the universal of gold, we have to go beyond our perceptions to more definitive properties, such as density and atomic number, which can be measured with scientific methodologies. From science, we know that gold has a unique atomic number (79) and a unique density (19.3 g/cm^3). Even though our senses might fool us sometimes, we can use scientific methodology to reach definitive conclusions about many of the objects in the world that we are unable to define precisely with sensation alone. In this way, Aristotle was correct to say universals inhere in the object, not in a nonmaterial realm of Forms or Ideas, and are independent of human perception or cognition—outside the mind.

Not all objects in the world are simple substances like gold with a unique density and atomic number, but we can use the same scientific process to identify other substances in the world, such as water (H2O) or sodium chloride AKA salt (NaCl), because material objects in the world are made of the basic building blocks of chemistry. The same idea applies to objects in the world that are more man-made and less natural, such as "escalator," "political party," and "brunch." The meanings of these universals depend to a great extent on the people who use these words, but the same rule applies in the sense of having precise definitions that allow us to distinguish them from all other things in the world. There is limited debate about the meaning of brunch, and it fits nicely with our practice of getting extra sleep on the weekend after working all week.

When we make the transition from inanimate matter to carbon-based life forms, such as humans, the process of finding the essence of individuals or species is more difficult but the same idea applies: if possible, look beyond sense perceptions to what can be verified independently. In the case of carbon-based life forms, rather than look to density or atomic numbers, we can look to DNA and the categories of zoology. Granted, the distinction between two species might not be as clear as the distinction between two elements on the periodic table, and we know that species evolve via genetic mutations, but if a trained scientist were to study a strand of DNA from an unidentified source, he should be able to identify the species without perceiving the living object. Granted, studying a strand of DNA will not tell us much about the nature of the living object, any more than we can know the content of a book written in a foreign language we do not understand, but this confirms Aristotle's insight that the essence of something is to be found in the material object (in this case, the DNA), not in the immaterial realm of Plato's Forms or Ideas or merely in the human mind. Better said: even if a universal exists in a nonmaterial realm of Forms or Ideas, we can also point to its existence in the material world.

The idea of breaking the world down into substances (objects in the world with a specific nature) and predicates (the qualities we perceive of these objects) was influential in the development of Aristotle's philosophy and its dominance into the Middle Ages, to the point where most of modern science and modern philosophy is, rightly or wrongly, viewed as a long process of agreeing or disagreeing with Aristotle. However, as Russell observed, most of the words in the dictionary besides nouns should also be thought of a universals, to include verbs and relations. In the case of verbs, some are visible in the natural world, such as "rain," "flow," or "erupt," whereas other verbs have a social context, such as "vote," "whisk," or "scribble," but we can treat them all as universals. In the case of relations, we should also consider universals like "inside of," "north of," or "greater than." This is important when comparing objects because it often leads to confusion. For example, if we have three brilliant people and rank them 1-3 based on their intelligence, this means 1 and 2 are smarter than 3. There is often a tendency to judge things by how they stacks up relative to other things, whereas it is often more important to judge something in and of itself. In a contest of three brilliant people, the person who gets third place is still brilliant, just as the person who graduates at the bottom of his medical school class is still a doctor. As was the case with other universals, in the case of relations, some are more natural than others and some are more man-made or specific to human activities.

Universals are important for political philosophy because they allow us to construct cohesive and consistent arguments that go beyond mere perception, and they allow us to achieve new levels of abstraction and complexity while maintaining a strong foundation and the overall integrity of our thought process—the narrow path. If we want to have a discussion about abstract ideas like rights and liberty, we cannot rely on our perceptions of colors, sounds, smells, and so on, and we cannot rely on vague uses of these terms. Rather, we need universals to help us ascend to new levels of abstract thought, with primary universals providing the foundation for more abstract universals, and so on. If our methodology is solid, then disagreement on the definition of universals should be the only thing in the way of people reaching consensus.

DEDUCTION

Most people reach conclusions on various issues, but most people do not take the time to think about their methodology to consider why they reach these conclusions. They just know, they claim, and often they are right, but often they are wrong. Just as most people employ complex grammar without thinking about it, because it is hard-wired into our brains after a certain age, most people can reach valid conclusions about issues without understanding the nuts and bolts of the methodology. They just know, they claim, and often they are right, but often they are wrong. As modern psychology has demonstrated, the human mind is riddled with biases and blind spots that often lead us down the path of false conclusions, often without our being aware. Therefore, if we are going to take the time to develop an effective web or hierarchy of universals to craft a political philosophy, we should take some time to think about how we think about different issues. In the case of deduction, it is a process of reasoning from statements to reach logically certain conclusions. In deduction, if our statements or premises are true, then the conclusion necessarily follows, and the process of analyzing statements to reach necessary conclusions is known as logic. If there are such things as necessary conclusions in political philosophy, we should do our best to find them.

The idea of necessary truth might sound odd. After all, can we ever be certain about anything? The answer is, yes, with an important caveat: assuming we are working with valid universals in the framework of logic. Consider the following argument:

Premise 1. Minneapolis is in Minnesota.

Premise 2. Minnesota is in the United States of America.

Conclusion. Minneapolis is in the United States of America.

There should be no debate about the meaning of Minneapolis, Minnesota, or the United States of America. Each term is a proper noun and is therefore not a universal, although "city," "state," and "country" are universals that help us understand the argument. By definition, universals represent a plurality of objects, and this plurality of objects is said to embody the universal. In this case, the argument hinges on the relational universal "in." As long as we all agree on the definition of this word ("in" means contained within something else) and it corresponds to something in reality, the conclusion necessarily follows from the two premises.

This was an easy example to show how we can use universals to achieve knowledge of the world and hold our thoughts together. To show the truth of this conclusion visually, we could make a point on a map where Minneapolis is located. Next, we could trace the border of Minnesota to show Minneapolis is in Minnesota. Finally, we could trace the border of the United States of America to show Minnesota is in the United States of America, which in turn would allow us to conclude that Minneapolis is in the United States of America. The critic might argue this methodology merely demonstrates what should be obvious to all and does not give us knowledge. We can see it is true; it is true by definition. However, if we were to use a similar process and extend it out 15-20 steps, such that we could no longer see the whole within our immediate grasp—think about a causal chain of evidence for a murder trial—it should be easy to see the power of deduction, both as a way to gain knowledge about the world and to expand the power our intellect. Not to mention, it is not clear why seeing truth makes it any less true.

To show a contrast, we should consider a deductive argument in which the definitions of the universals are open to debate but the conclusions follows necessarily from the premises:

Premise 1. All women possess the theoretical capacity to have children.

Premise 2. All people who possess the theoretical capacity to have children should be barefoot and pregnant in the kitchen.

Conclusion. All women should be barefoot and pregnant in the kitchen.

I have no doubt that most people disagree with this conclusion, but the interesting part is that the conclusion follows necessarily from the premises. How is this possible? If logic is the science of reaching necessary conclusions from premises, how is it possible to construct valid yet false arguments? Once again, back to universals. Logic works only if the universals are valid, just like a computer works only if we program it correctly. Logic is a mental framework, the laws of thought, for working with components of an argument—after we have taken the time to ensure the components are valid. Again, the fact we can use a machete to open a coconut does not mean we should use it to open someone's head. To gain knowledge of the world, we require universals, but with the added complexity of fitting them into a valid framework so we can use them properly. Without universals, we will never transcend our fleeting perceptions and will remain trapped in the fiery world of Heraclitus and subsistence farming. People who argue for relativism have to use universals to deny the existence of universals.

Mathematics is a good example of deduction. The rules of mathematics are similar to the rules of logic, but rather than rely on premises, mathematicians speak about axioms, which are self-evident truths that cannot be proven by other means. Axioms are the bedrock that provides the foundation for the truths of mathematics, combined with rules of the game (addition, subtraction, multiplication, division, exponent, and so on). Consider the case of geometric proofs, which rely on axioms regarding parallel lines or the shortest distance between two points. We can use these truths to prove other truths in geometry, but we cannot prove the axioms. They are the result of intuitive insight. The axioms of mathematics are supposed to be so obvious and irrefutable that no one should be able to conclude otherwise, but this does not explain how the insight is possible. Can we imagine a two-dimensional plane in which parallel lives ever cross? Of course we cannot. In many ways, this axiom could be said to be true by definition: we shall define parallel lines as any two lines that never cross in a two-dimensional plane, which makes axioms less mysterious.

Turning to arithmetic, the reason everyone agrees 2 + 2 = 4 is because everyone agrees on the definitions of the terms and the rules of the game. If we agree on what we mean by 2 and +, then the conclusion 4 follows necessarily, which makes this a deductive thought process. However, as the findings of mathematical philosophy have shown, this does not mean mathematics can be reduced to logic; in fact, Gödel's incompleteness theorems prove it is impossible to reduce mathematics to logic. Some people have no trouble with the idea of axioms, but many people find it troubling to hear mathematics is grounded on axioms that cannot be proved. What if the axioms are wrong? Have we discovered all of them? As it turns out, there is limited debate about the meaning of the terms of mathematics, which is why there is limited debate about the conclusions of mathematics. One notable exception is the Axiom of Infinity in Set Theory, which presumes the existence of a set that contains an actual infinity of members. There is not universal agreement on infinity, and many people would argue that whether an infinite set exists is the heart of the matter and cannot be assumed away with an axiom. In this case, the Axiom of Infinity begs the question.

The most important point about deduction is we must arrive at the universals we use in deductive arguments by means of intuition or induction, just as we do with the axioms of mathematics. To the extent that intuition or induction breaks down, deduction breaks down as well. The truths of a deductive argument necessarily follow from the premises or axioms, but the challenging part is reaching agreement on the premises or axioms. Some universals are more difficult to define than others and some can be verified by independent means, but many of the disagreements we see in political philosophy boil down to the fact that people cannot agree on universals. In some cases, one person might make a logical error, which is easy to remedy, but more often than not the different parties cannot reach agreement on the definitions of the universals. What is a *right*? What is *justice*? What is *fairness*? What is an *investment*? We quickly find ourselves in a Platonic dialog being pestered by Socrates to define our terms.

Shifting to political philosophy, there are two areas where the deductive method has played an important role: scripture and the rule of law. In the case of scripture, the methodology for believers is deductive. People who believe scripture believe the truths contained in scripture are valid and can be used as premises or axioms to reach conclusions about how to live in the world, just as the axioms of geometry can be used in proofs. The major difference is that whereas the axioms of geometry are assumed to be obvious to anyone who takes the time to consider them, the axioms of scripture are not always intuitive because the fundamental idea of scripture is humans are incapable of intuiting the highest truths on their own and therefore need divine revelation to open our minds. If the axioms of scripture were obvious, we would not need scripture. The important point of scripture, rightly or wrongly, is it addresses issues we know we will never be able to answer with the power of human reason alone. Given that scripture is often difficult to interpret and given that people often pick and choose which passages to use as axioms, we open ourselves up to the possibility of reaching invalid or inconsistent conclusions via logically valid means.

In the case of rule of law, such as a constitution or laws, we are also working with a deductive system. As is the case with all axioms or universals, we rely on intuitive or inductive processes to arrive at constitutions or laws, but once the ink dries, constitutions or laws should serve as the foundation for deductive reasoning within the legal system, with a mechanism to amend the constitution that requires reasonable consensus. Otherwise, why go through the process of making constitutions? No legal system can capture every nuance of human life, and there will always be room for interpretation and discretion, hence the idea of Common Law, but a legal system works only if it is taken as providing the axiomatic foundation for making decisions. For example, to determine whether a man should be charged with the crime of assault, we have to compare the definition of assault to what a court can prove the person did based on the evidence. There might be disagreement on what constitutes assault and what the punishment should be for a conviction, and our definitions and standards might change over time, but it does not make sense to raise those points in a courtroom. The job of lawyers and judges is to operate within the legal framework as written and leave any modifications of the legal system (reworking the axioms) to the legislative branch. Surprisingly, this is often a source of contention—people not understanding or accepting that our legal system is inherently deductive. We have all seen cases where senators ask supreme court nominees whether they think a law or ruling is right or wrong, and receive the only correct response, which is that judges should interpret the laws and the constitution as written, even if it means ruling against their personal convictions or contrary to their beliefs about right and wrong.

INDUCTION

If deduction is the process of reasoning from statements containing universals to reach logically certain conclusions containing the same universals, induction is the process of reasoning from particular statements containing universals to more general statements containing higher order or more abstract universals, such as the transition from a falling apple to a universal law of gravity. The important distinction between deduction and induction is that with induction the conclusion goes beyond the information in the particulars and does not necessarily follow from the particulars. We are making a broader generalization based on the evidence. For example, a syllogism in the previous section included two premises that included three terms: Minneapolis, Minnesota, and the United States of America. Based on the relationship of the middle term, Minnesota, to the other two terms, we were able to make a certain conclusion regarding the relationship between Minneapolis and the United States of America based on the universal "in." We learned something new that was not explicit in the premises, but this something new was implicit in the premises.

Whereas the challenge with deduction is defining our universals to the satisfaction of as many people as possible, because the conclusions follow necessarily, the challenge with induction is interpreting the data to reach conclusions that satisfy most people. Consider the relationship between capital punishment and murder rates, or the relationship between marriage and income, or the relationship between education and likelihood to vote. The data are available for all to see, but many people have preconceived beliefs that shape how they respond to the data or how they filter out the data that do not fit their mold. Even for people who have no dog in the fight or are genuinely open to finding the truth, people often reach different conclusions. To make matters worse, even if we can reach consensus on the data, there will often be disagreement on what policies should be implemented to address the challenge. For example, even if we can prove capital punishment has a negligible impact on deterring crime, some will argue that people who commit murder deserve to die for their crime, on principle, regardless of whether the punishment deters other people from committing murder. The punishment is designed for the individual, not for society, according to this perspective.

Needless to say, the most heated disagreements in political philosophy are grounded in induction, not deduction, both because different groups seek out data to support their arguments and because the conclusions go beyond the data to more abstract universals like rights, justice, and fairness. If we have clear axioms, there should be no debate about the conclusions in the case of deduction. In the case of induction, however, as we climb to new levels of abstraction we face two challenges. First, humans are not inanimate objects, like the objects of physics, which means it is more difficult to make general statements about human behavior in the way we develop the laws of physics. Second, our hopes and dreams, rational or irrational, shape the process. In many cases, people believe their vision for how society should be is more important than the evidence. Just as some people look for no evidence to support their faith, some people promote political philosophies even if they know it would be impossible to implement such a system or that every attempted to implement it in history has had disastrous consequences.

The most common form of induction is the numerical or statistical method, whereby the more often something happens, the more justified we are in reaching a general conclusion. For example, if the sun rises every day in the east and has done so for thousands of years of recorded history—or, better said, if we have never seen an instance to the contrary—we can state with a higher degree of confidence over time that the sun will rise in the east tomorrow. Such a methodology naturally gives rise to the concept of causality: the universe displays predictable uniformity. Knowing what we know about the universe—the rotation of earth, its orbit around the sun, gravity, and so on—we can imagine a sequence of causal events that will result in the sun rising in the east tomorrow. I believe most people would not give this claim about the sun rising in the east a second thought, but influential philosophers like Hume have asked the law of causality for its credentials, even though his own language was riddled with causal reasoning. If we accept Hume's claim that empirical data alone provides the basis for knowledge, then he was correct to take a critical look at causality; however, if we hope to achieve scientific knowledge about the universe, we have to accept, one way or another, induction and causality. Granted, we might not be able to identify a specific cause or understand exactly what is happening at a subatomic level, but our ability to predict events in nature suggests that belief in causality is reasonable.

Philosophers and scientists have struggled with the problem of induction for centuries. If repeated events merely increase the probability of truth and there is nothing logically contradictory about events happening otherwise (the earth in theory could begin rotating the other way), can we ever achieve true knowledge via induction? Or, for our purposes, do we have a systematic way to achieve precise definitions of abstract universals like rights, justice, and fairness? The answer is it is not possible if we make the assumption that knowledge has to be irrefutable or absolute like mathematics. Consider a rock breaking a piece of glass. Rather than focus on the perception of the rock smashing through the glass, we could dig deeper and investigate variables such as the size of the rock, the weight of the rock, the velocity of the rock, the size of the glass, the thickness of the glass, and so on. Some rocks break glass and others do not, but we know enough about rocks and glass to know, often with precision, when a particular rock will break a particular piece of glass. In other words, there is something specific about the nature of rocks and glass that allows us to make accurate predictions. For example, if a fifty pound spherical piece of granite is dropped from the top of the Leaning Tower of Pisa to a 6' x 6' piece of glass one centimeter thick suspended two feet above the ground by table legs at each corner, the glass will break 100% of the time. Granted, perceptions alone will not prove this to us, because we can always imagine the piece of granite bouncing off the glass, but by exploiting the power of universals, we can often make inductive claims about the world with the confidence of deduction.

Shifting gears to humans, even though we possess varying degrees of freewill and are not bound by the laws of nature in the same way that rocks and glass are, we can still investigate who we are in terms of our biological growth and maturity to make general statements about how we should behave and how we should structure our society to help us fulfill our potential in a sustainable way, meaning from one generation to the next. If we can predict when a rock will break a piece of glass, we can often predict how people on average will behave when exposed to different stimuli. For example, if children are properly loved, nourished, and educated, we can promote positive behavior and reduce the probability of negative behavior, all things being equal on a bell curve kind of way. The reason for this is that humans have a nature, a teleology, which should be taken into consideration when developing a political philosophy. When people behave in predictable ways, it is because they have teleology, not because they lack freewill. The material world shapes the kind of people we become and what kind of society we have, but this is due primarily to human nature and only secondarily to the material world, just as a rose seed becomes a rose, regardless of the material environment. A bad environment will limit the ability of the rose to fulfill its rose potential, but a bad environment will never cause a rose seed to grow into daisy. The important point is if we introduce the idea of teleology, it allows us to solve the problem of induction in political philosophy, for reasons I will address in the next chapter.

A PRIORI KNOWLEDGE

Although science is focused on drawing conclusions from empirical evidence—gaining knowledge via induction—scientific progress also depends on intuition. In fact, scientific method calls on us to propose a hypothesis prior to collecting evidence, as well as to define what evidence will support or discredit our hypothesis. How is this possible? Granted, a scientist with a long history of collecting and analyzing empirical data will develop his power of intuition to think with greater precision and efficiency, but the fact remains a scientific hypothesis will precede the evidence, which in turn raises questions about how such intuitive insights are possible.

Although a scientific hypothesis should, in theory, be limited to what can be confirmed or denied by the evidence, some of the most important scientific theories, such as quantum theory or string theory, are based on intuitions, which might never be proved one way or another due to lack of evidence. To this extent, the lines between science and philosophy have blurred because philosophy deals with establishing intellectual systems that go beyond the evidence, but some scientists seem to be dipping their toes into the philosophical waters as well. Granted, philosophy will always take its cues from science—most academic disciplines were considered part of philosophy before going solo—but philosophy has to go beyond the empirical evidence to have any value as an independent discipline. In the case of political philosophy, we can look to the evidence to shape policy in a developed country, such as the marginal rate of return on education spending, but it takes philosophical insight to discern the patterns of what a society should do over time to progress to modern state status. The empirical evidence will leave clues to these patterns, but it will never give us the entire map. For this, we require the intellect, intuition, and philosophy.

One of the most important questions of philosophy, perhaps the most important question, is whether synthetic *a priori* knowledge is possible, to coin a term from Kant. By synthetic *a priori* we mean prior to experience (not the result of empirical evidence) and in a way that tells us something new about the world (not true merely by definition). Many people in the modern world have come to accept the idea that all knowledge is grounded in experience alone, which is taught by a school of philosophy called empiricism. However, the history of philosophy has also been influenced by scholasticism and rationalism, which in different ways argue that although knowledge comes from experience, the intellect is capable of gaining knowledge by means of abstraction or innate ideas. This debate between empiricists and rationalists has been important in modern philosophy, with the empiricists focused on empirical data and induction and the rationalists focused on innate ideas and deduction. Extreme rationalists like Plato focused on the eternal One of Parmenides, and extreme empiricists like Hume focused on the fleeting fire of Heraclitus, but as I have attempted to show in this book, the correct answer takes both of these views into consideration—the one and the many. If we consider that science and philosophy are not possible with pure empiricism, which some empiricists admit, then we have to accept that the intellect is capable of acquiring some knowledge in ways that are not wholly dependent on perception, in ways I do not claim to understand. The intellect does this via intuition and the universals it creates, but we should investigate what it means to say we have knowledge prior to experience that tells us something about the world.

As Russell observed, *a priori* knowledge deals with the relations of universals. For example, if Minneapolis is in Minnesota and Minnesota is in the United States of America, then Minneapolis is in the United States of America. To speak more generally, if x is in y and y is in z, then x is in z. This statement is true in all possible circumstances—we know this truth *a priori*—as long as we all agree on the universal "in." Therefore, armed with this knowledge, we can look for circumstances where this formula applies. If we find three places or objects such that the first is in the second and the second is in the third, then the first is in the third. The same goes for our discussion of a rock breaking a piece of glass. Depending on the size, weight, and speed of a rock, we can predict with precision whether it will break a piece of glass of a specific size and thickness.

To speak more generally and scientifically, if one object with a particular force—Force = mass x acceleration (F = ma)—strikes another object that is incapable of resisting the force of the first object, the second object will break, by definition, 100% of the time. Thus, we have a way to know in advance what will happen in the real world before we perceive the activity. If we turn on the right filters to eliminate what is not relevant for a particular issue (rock, glass, etc.) and focus on what matters (the force of the first object and the capacity of the second object to resist force), we can know in advance (*a priori*) what will happen when two objects collide, even if we have never seen two such objects collide in the past. This does not mean the world does not contain particular objects like rocks and glass; it means we can abstract relevant variables from these objects that make the particular qualities and predicates of these objects irrelevant, at least in the context of science. One of the problems with stripping away the qualities of the world and reducing the world only to what is quantifiable, however, is qualities still exist and play a critical role in understanding humans and political philosophy.

To the extent that we can gain knowledge this way, there is some truth to the claim of the scholastics or rationalists that some knowledge is possible without experience, as defined by the empiricists, even if all knowledge begins with experience. Experience might prime the pump (the mind) to begin the process of abstraction, but the perceptions of the empirical world alone are insufficient to account for the vast complexities of human knowledge. As far as how this is possible, a rationalist like Descartes or Leibniz would argue the mind has innate ideas that naturally blossom and take their correct position in our web or hierarchy of concepts if we educate our minds properly. For this reason, the rationalists focused on reaching pure ideas by intuition (like axioms) and then using them in a deductive way to gain knowledge about the world. They were less focused on perception and induction. This process can be taken too far, such as when logic takes priority over causality, such as with the philosophy of Spinoza, but the mysterious powers of the intellect and intuition remain.

One of the most interesting solutions offered for the problem of *a priori* knowledge was from Kant, who addressed the issue in the *Critique of Pure Reason*, which is widely considered one of the most important books in modern philosophy. Whether Kant was right or wrong, the process of understand his philosophy and seeing the world through his eyes is a challenging and rewarding intellectual exercise. In short, Kant said synthetic *a priori* knowledge is possible because our minds shape perceptions in accordance with the forms of the intellect. For example, the reason we perceive the world within the framework of time and space is because the intellect is structured to present sense data to us within the framework of time and space. According to Kant, whereas the traditional way of thinking how we acquire knowledge is for our minds to conform to the objects of reality, Kant argued the objects of reality conform to our minds, a paradigm shift Kant compared to a Copernican revolution whereby humans came to understand the earth revolves around the sun, not the other way, even though the movement of the sun looks the same regardless of which view we accept.

To use an example, if we play a DVD movie, the DVD player will present a two-dimensional movie with sights and sounds on the television. There is nothing inherent in the digital ones and zeros on the DVD that would suggest sights and sounds on a television to someone who had no idea what he is looking at. It might make sense to talk about a correspondence between the digital ones and zeros and what we see and hear on the television (which presumes the existence of an algorithm or intellect to bridge the gap), but the DVD player was designed to present raw data on the television as two-dimensional images with sounds. According to Kant, the same goes for humans. We cannot get to the reality behind our perceptions (the thing-in-itself or *Ding an sich*), but we can have knowledge of the perceptions our intellect plays a key role in shaping.

CONCLUSION

Universals make up the majority of the words in the dictionary and come in the form of the parts of grammar—nouns, adjectives, prepositions, and so on. Our ability to create or discover them and work with them is grounded in the fact that we are rational creatures, and the fact that they are grounded in reality makes knowledge possible. Universals are not proper nouns, like names and cities. They are abstractions from reality that exist in a plurality of objects, but they also require the power of the human intellect to reach their full potential of refinement and definition. Some universals are better than others, like the transition from the model of the four elements (earth, air, fire, and water) of ancient Greece to the elements of the periodic table of modern chemistry, but less refined universals will often work with a modest degree of success if they are grounded in reality.

In a world that appears to be in a constant state of change, universals are the steppingstones in the flux that allow us to stay on the narrow path without inadvertently taking the exit ramps for the changeless world of Parmenides or the perpetual flux of Heraclitus. Languages change over time, but this does not mean truth is relative; and we can talk about refining our universals to achieve enough clarity in our definitions to please Socrates. Universals are critical to our analysis of political philosophy because universals provide the intellectual framework of our system. As our analysis continues, we will see that many of the conflicts in political philosophy often boil down to disagreements about universals.

CHAPTER TWO. SO BELOW

A common approach to philosophy is dividing the focus of our analysis into the outer world of perception and the inner world of reflection, to include how the two worlds are related and shape each other. In this case, our approach to the outer world focuses on physical objects like rocks, animals, weather, and planets, and our approach to the inner world focuses on mental phenomena like feelings, passions, morals, and motivations.

Universals exist in the outer and inner realms. Love is no less of a universal than gold, but the definition of gold is clear and objective whereas the definition of love is less clear and more subjective, which is not to say we will never reach an objective definition of love. All people who have ever experienced love know love is real, but if love as a universal is ever to rise above the level of a vague intuition or the fluttering of our hearts, we have to develop a definition with an acceptable degree of objectivity, in ways that would cause some people to recognize that what they thought was love was something else, such as lust, or would cause some people to recognize that what they thought was not love was love after all, like a man and a woman in a romantic comedy who think they hate each other but realize they love each other. One of the best ways to add clarity to the definition of love is to recognize there are different types of love—love of a parent, love of a spouse, love of a child, love of a friend, love of a country, and so on. Just as we should not allow the often fleeting and vague nature of our inner world prevent us from deriving clear inner world universals, we should not allow an unnecessarily general universal like love prevent us from making legitimate distinctions, such as confusing the love a man has for the mother of his children for the love the same man has for a childhood friend.

One of the most important factors to consider when reflecting on the inner world is that the feelings, passions, morals, and motivations we experience subjectively have an objective, outer world foundation. We can study the physiology and chemistry of love, but we can also talk about what it is like to experience love. This does not mean love can be reduced to physiology or chemistry, because positive or negative thoughts can shape our physiology and chemistry, but we can say particular feelings, passions, morals, and motivations will be accompanied by predictable patterns in our physiology and chemistry, and vice versa, such that we can talk about natural feelings, passions, morals, and motivations. For example, the physiological and chemical activity that tends to accompany the adrenaline rush of skydiving is not the same physiological and chemical activity that tends to accompany depression.

The inner world seems more vague and chaotic than the outer world, but we should remember the outer world seemed vague and chaotic to the earliest people, until they developed scientific insight and understanding of the outer world to make sense of it. I am not saying we will one day develop our understanding of the inner world with the precision of billiard balls colliding in space, like physics, in part because this would contradict the widely accepted and credible belief in freewill, but some of the vagueness and chaos of the inner world is the result of a lack of maturity and refinement, and some of the vagueness and chaos can be resolved with a scientific approach. For now, the important point is our biological growth and maturity is not vague or random, and we can track our biological growth and maturity in ways that allow us to make decisions about how to live, and how not to live, if we aspire to arrive at maturity, happiness, and fulfillment.

To set the stage for a discussion of teleology, we should review our analysis of causality. Whereas we can say all events have a cause, even if we do not know what the cause is—we can talk about the uniformity of nature—we should recognize there are different types of causes. For example, if a billiard ball is struck by another billiard ball before rolling into a corner pocket, this is different from the cause that moves a flower to blossom or a person to grow taller. Modern science tends to focus on using mathematical models to describe the activity of inanimate objects colliding in space, devoid of any qualitative considerations, but the growth, maturity, and decay of organic objects is no less a causal sequence of events.

Aristotle, who played an important role in the establishment of biology as a science, was no stranger to the importance of organic causality, and it played an important role in his theory of the four causes: material, formal, efficient, and final. To repeat a common example, consider a statue. The material cause is the marble; the formal cause is the plan or design that shapes the project; the efficient cause is the sculptor with the hammer and the chisel doing the work; and the final cause is the final result, which in many ways shapes the whole process because the artist measures his progress against his vision of the final product. As a conceptual model this is reasonable, but Aristotle believed it captured what was happening below the surface in the world, such as arguing that the formal cause of humans naturally steers them toward the final cause of humans performing actions in accordance with virtue and philosophical reflection.

What Aristotle means by this is all things in the world have a natural end, or *telos*, toward which they naturally strive, which is easy to misinterpret, especially in the case of inanimate objects. Hot air does not "strive" to rise but it rises necessarily due to the laws of science. To understand Aristotle, it is critical to understand what he means by formal and final causes because they provide the foundation for his doctrines of potential versus actual and teleology, the latter of which I will develop in this chapter. The history of modern science has moved in the direction of ignoring or rejecting formal and final causes by reducing the activity of the world to mathematical formulas, thus reducing science to material and efficient causes; but as we will see, especially in the case of organic life, we are missing the big picture and the qualitative aspects of life that are important to human life if we eliminate formal and final causes from the discussion.

THE INDIVIDUAL

One of the keys to understanding teleology is to keep our ideas grounded in reality long enough to build a solid foundation for higher levels of abstraction. Just as organized religion often gets a bad rap, for the right and wrong reasons, so does teleology, which is often dismissed as an ancient or medieval relic that injected too much mysticism into science. Before we make any lofty speculations on the final cause of man (there is no shortage of them in the history of political philosophy, on the left and the right), we should focus our efforts on finding the foundational bricks that would make such an abstract leap possible and reasonable, in accordance with the evidence.

We should therefore begin with the basics, like nutrition, which Aristotle addressed as the lowest form of the soul (his use of the word soul did not have the same meaning it has today). For most of human history, people have had to scrounge for their next meal, eating anything that habit or custom suggested would not kill them, or even resorting to war to plunder the food, treasure, and women of other tribes. Even today, hundreds and millions of people struggle with life at this basic level of existence, with malnutrition and obesity the most common outcomes of poor diet and lack of exercise. If we make the systematic transition from foraging to the universals of agriculture and livestock, we should be able to establish a science of diet that will keep us on the optimal path of biological growth and maturity. If we agree that healthy thoughts follow from a healthy body, our control variable will be people with proper nourishment, which is not to say all people with a healthy body have healthy thoughts or that all people with an unhealthy body have unhealthy thoughts. All things being equal, the claim that people should strive to provide proper nutrition for their bodies should have bipartisan support.

The first step is to identify the essential nutrients (universals)— proteins, carbohydrates, fats, vitamins, minerals, water, etc.—and focus less attention on the specific foods. It might be true that turkey and broccoli are good for our health, but the reality is high quality proteins, fats, and carbohydrates are good for our health, especially when they are fresh, taken in the right proportions, and loaded with vitamins and minerals. Based on our age, weight, and activity level, we can talk about an optimal diet. Our biological growth and development depends on what we eat and drink, to the extent that a failure to consume the right nutrients in the right quantities will result in suboptimal growth. If the brain needs certain nutrients to develop properly, then the absence of those nutrients will prevent the brain from developing to its full potential.

It should surprise no one with respect for science that mother's breast milk is just what the doctor ordered for infants, and we as a society should actively promote and provide incentives for the consumption of mother's breast milk for all infants to give them best chance of fulfilling their potential. (To my dismay, gender politics has inserted itself into this topic to label breastfeeding a form of male oppression for what should be considered the most obvious scientific fact for infant nutrition.) After that, nature leaves it up to us to figure out the correct way to eat and drink, first via trial and error, and later via the science of diet, which requires universals. Granted, the body is resilient and can survive long periods of malnutrition, but all things being equal in a bell curve kind of way, making sure people consume the right diet should be the first step to help people, as much as possible, fulfill their teleology.

People in polite company are advised to avoid discussing religion or politics. To that list, to my surprise, I would add diet. Despite all the science we have for nutrition, there is significant disagreement on what we should eat and drink, evidenced by all the diet books and fads. The professional consensus is that things like tobacco, alcohol, and processed sugars are not good for us, and focusing on what not to consume is a useful technique, but the disagreement over meat and protein is peculiar. A review of our physiology, from our forward-looking eyes to our canine teeth and the structure of our digestive track, should leave no doubt for anyone with even a modest respect for science that we are designed to eat and digest meat, in addition to other food—we are omnivores. High quality protein and fat are essential for brain development, and yet people with a straight face will tell us as a blanket statement that eating meat is bad for us.

Granted, it is possible to eat too much meat and some meats are better than others, especially if they are combined with unhealthy foods like soda and French fries, but meat and protein should be an essential part of any diet. I am always troubled to hear about parents who impose vegetarian or vegan diets on their children. Just as communities should intervene to ensure all children get a good education, communities should intervene to ensure all children get sufficient protein. I am obviously not proposing criminal consequences for these parents, but public health announcements and social dialog would not be out of line. My experience with vegetarians or vegans is they tend to have either a moral aversion to eating animals (often because of how the animals are killed, which often is appalling) or they believe consuming animals is bad for the environment because of the resources required to produce one pound of meat. Rarely have I heard a vegetarian say protein itself is not healthy; even the most die-hard vegetarians look for ways to supplement their diets with protein. The fact that vegetarian or vegan diets cannot succeed without protein supplements should tell us something about how the human body evolved over millions of years. Our ancestors did not have the luxury of protein powder. The fact that so much contention exists at the scientifically objective level of diet should demonstrate why it is so difficult to achieve consensus in political philosophy, and why any continued shift to a sugar or carbohydrate-heavy diet, either by choice or due to lack of wealth, will only exasperate the diabetes epidemic.

Just as Aristotle made the transition from plant-like nutrition to animal-like motion, we should now make the transition to the science of physical activity as it relates to our teleology. It was no accident the Greeks considered gymnastics essential to our biological growth and maturity, especially for children. And just as we can talk about a correct diet, we can also talk about correct activity or motion. Given the nature of our organism—muscles, bones, heart, respiratory system, circulatory system, and so on—we can talk about activity with a net benefit for our health. We have to work our muscles to a certain point of failure to make them grow; we have to raise our heartbeat to the right level for a sustained time to get an aerobic benefit; we have to stretch our muscles and tendons to the right point to maintain flexibility and avoid injury, and so on.

We as a culture seem to have accepted this, but the epidemic of obesity or the culture of sitting around watching television or playing video game speaks otherwise. When I was a child, the challenge of most parents where I lived was tracking down their kids to eat dinner or go to bed. If we were not riding our bikes, skateboarding, or playing football, we were talking about new things to do. Now the challenge seems to be getting children out of the house or finding ways to have fun without a schedule or not arranged by parents. There also seems to be a tendency for parents with "gifted" children to believe gym or sports are not essential to growth and maturity. Granted, not all children are born to play professional sports, but we are organic creatures and activity is essential to our growth and maturity. We learn about ourselves and grind ourselves to new levels of refinement with physical activity.

Finally, when we transition to education and the development of the mind, there is no shortage of disagreement in ways that have a profound impact on political philosophy. The rise of charter schools, home schooling, and school vouchers show that education is one of the most contentious areas where the rubber meets the road in political philosophy. The most important detail is by the time we begin educating our children, much of the positive investment or damage has already been done. Education should be designed to keep us on the narrow path and to unlearn the bad habits that keep us off the narrow path, but all things being equal, children who come from broken homes with a poor diet and limited physical activity will be at a significant disadvantage, which is why calls to improve inner city high schools is often too little too late. This is why I raised diet and activity before education. In many ways, the game of life begins before conception. We cannot choose our parents, but our parent's choices, such as finishing school, getting married, working, or avoiding substance abuse, play a critical role in shaping our future.

Shifting back to education, we have to look at it from two perspectives: our moral education and our practical education. A liberal arts education exposes us to the glorious history of the arts and sciences, with the goal of making us well-rounded individuals who are capable critical thinking, living meaningful lives, and making positive contributions to society. Whereas some have argued that humans living in a state of perpetual war are living in a state of nature, I would argue that people with refined intellects and artistic talents are living in a state of nature, to the extent that we are living in accordance with the potential that exists within each of us. Our fulfilled nature is our true nature. Thus, when we think about a traditional liberal arts education, we should think of it not as a luxury but as an important part of our biological growth and maturity, with the understanding that most people, for a variety of reasons, will fall short.

Likewise, to live a fulfilling life, each person should find a practical skill that will allow him to make a living by creating things or services other people value and are willing to pay for. Our current educational system fails at both. Many people are leaving high school or college with a limited knowledge of history, literature, and philosophy, and with even more limited knowledge in terms of practical job skills. The want ads are filled with jobs for nurses, accountants, IT specialists, and other jobs for skilled labor, but the coffee shops and restaurants are filled with baristas and waiters who studied something else with student loans weighing them down. Many people do not have the luxury of dedicating themselves to a liberal arts education, and they might not want to go to a trade school for fear of the (unfortunate) stigma associated with not having a college degree. Sadly, by making a college degree a box-checking exercise, we have reduced the value of it by lowering standards and flooding the market with college graduates into an economy that cannot absorb them all.

The best we can do is ensure children are taught the right things at the right times during their biological growth and maturity. In most cases, a piece of chalk and a blackboard will suffice. Inner city schools might have less funding than wealthy schools in the suburbs, but it costs less money to give children challenging math assignments and hold them accountable for their homework than it does to buy computers to surf the Internet for research projects. If children are required to read for one or two hours every day, they will learn to read. If they are required to memorize their multiplication charts every day, they will lean to multiply. I once visited a school in India where young girls, many of whom were poor by American standards, were doing calculus in high school, with enthusiastic hands going up each time I asked a question. It can be done, and at a much lower cost than what we are paying today.

The important point is we should train children how to think, not what to think. The brain is like a muscle that learns from repetition and intensity, in much the same way the body learns to perform actions. Only after our brains have developed to a reasonable degree of maturity and refinement does it make sense to talk about putting information into our minds. A failure to understand our teleology—in this case, how we learn—is leaving many children at a disadvantage, in particular, the people with the fewest advantages. If we are serious about education, we should consider how the wealthiest families educate their children in private schools, which undoubtedly includes less obsessing about self-esteem and more obsessing about discipline and hard work. Just as no one would expect to make the Olympic team without a grueling training program over many years, the same should be said for education. Our brains develop and mature in such a way that we should be taught the right things at the right time and in the right intensity, with the understanding that if done properly, most children will struggle with school and dream of a day it ends. Children should not hate school, but if they love it too much, they are probably being pandered to rather than being genuinely challenged.

Most of the topics I raised in this section are empirical and within the realm of the sciences, which is why I focused less on specific ideas and more on general ideas. The key point is we are organic creatures that grow and mature according to scientific principles. In theory, an obese couch potato who drops out of high school could become successful, depending on how we define success, but just as the most beautiful roses benefit from soil, sunlight, and water, it does not make sense to talk about fulfilling our teleological potential unless we are acting in accordance with the laws of science. History is filled with examples of people who deliberately deny their physical bodies, often in an ascetic or religious context, to show the predominance of the soul or spirit over the body, but the problem also goes the other way with people who indulge their physical bodies without limit to deny the existence of a soul or spirit.

Just as we look to science when determining the best way to plant our crops, we should look to science to find the best way to nurture the growth and maturity of our organism. As a final point, although we need universals and science to determine what we need in terms of diet, exercise, and education, this is the easy part. Anyone can say kids need x, y, and z to increase their chances for success. We already know this. Far more difficult is structuring our society— political philosophy—in such a way as to produce these resources in a sustainable way.

SOCIETY

A common criticism of religion is it supposedly stems from a primitive way of thinking that projects the mysteries of the inner world onto the outer world or invokes supernatural causes when natural causes will do just fine. Mystics often speak about the correspondence between the macrocosm (outer world) and the microcosm (inner world). For example, because people have an innate sense of justice—we are hard-wired for justice (which I will address in chapter seven)—we conclude the universe also must be governed by justice, such as the law of karma, which means an all-powerful God must exist to enforce this justice. Or, given that justice apparently can never be fully achieved in this lifetime, there must be an afterlife where good people finally receive justice in heaven and bad people finally receive justice in hell. The list could continue, but although this could be considered a valid criticism of a particular methodology of thinking, this does not mean the ideas themselves are flawed (justice, God, etc.). This type of flawed criticism is known as the genetic fallacy and is defined by judging ideas based on their origins rather than their merits. As we saw in the section on deduction, some people reach the right conclusions for the wrong reasons or the wrong conclusions for the right reasons, and we are equally justified in looking at the problem from the other perspective: perhaps the reason people are hard-wired for justice with a belief in the afterworld is because we are a reflection of the world, not the other way. Therefore, just as a less refined mind might reach a valid conclusion via a flawed methodology, a more refined mind might reach the same valid conclusion via a valid methodology.

Stepping down from the rungs of theology, there are valid ways to look at how we project our inner world onto the outer world, in particular, onto society. We can go back to Plato to see a system in which the inner world or psychology of the individual was projected onto society. According to Plato, the inner world or psychology of humans has three components: reason, spirit (ambition), and appetite. Just as the four elements—earth, air, water, and fire—represented a crude yet partially true view of the world, so was Plato's view of our inner world or psychology. We know today that the reality of human psychology is more complex, but this does not mean Plato's system is incapable of any truths or insights.

Truth or falsity aside, the important point was Plato took this inner world model and projected it onto the outer world of society as a model for how we should live with each other. Just as reason, spirit (ambition), and appetite are the guiding forces of our inner world, Plato thought they should also be the guiding forces or structure of our society, at least in reference to the City States of ancient Greece. Therefore, society needs some people (the majority) to focus on managing the appetites of society (food, commerce, etc.), which is the lowest social class of the merchants. Next, we need some people to focus on managing the spirit (ambition) of society, which is the next higher class of warriors. Finally, we need a small number of elites to focus on managing the reason of society, which takes us to the highest class of philosopher kings called the Guardians, who rule over society with authority and wisdom. Plato's often shocking blueprint for an authoritarian government in the *Republic* has sparked the imagination of many well intentioned philosophers throughout the ages, especially people who probably fancied themselves would-be members of the Guardian class.

Although we can talk about humans as autonomous entities that are capable of surviving on their own, humans are social creatures by nature and are most likely to reach their full potential in a community that allows them to specialize in their work and share the burden. As Aristotle observed, any person who is unable to live in society or has no need for society, because he is self-sufficient, is either a beast or a god. Our true nature is such that as we achieve our full potential and fulfill our teleology, we are less capable of living on our own, especially in a modern state. Someone who dedicates his life to managing nuclear power plants probably would not last long on a deserted island. In fact, we could make the argument that modern states require people to specialize in their work to such a degree that people become dependent on each other in ways that is not the case in a less developed society, thus linking the division of labor to social progress and the rise of the modern state.

Granted, there is something to be said for people "getting back to nature" and learning survival skills to live off the land, but if we want to live in a modern state that benefits from technology and the arts, we need an education system that sets people on the path of specialization for a division of labor that goes beyond basic survival skills. To the extent we create a society of people who specialize in enough unique skills such that we can tap into the full potential of our organism (food, shelter, safety, education, art, science, and so on), we are projecting our teleology onto society. However, rather than projecting the actual components of our inner world, such as Plato's reason, spirit (ambition), and appetite, we are projecting the social functions and institutions that are required for us to achieve our potential.

If we can talk about society as an organism, with people performing individual roles in support of the collective whole, then we need to clarify our terms to see how this thinking applies to humans. On the one hand, if we consider ants or bees we see a population that appears to be working as a collective whole in which each ant or bee plays a specific role that is defined by birth. Most important, these ants and bees do not give a second thought to their roles, do not aspire to perform different roles, and often are prepared to give their life for the sake of the community, without fanfare or recognition. On some level, this idea of a social organism appeals to some people. On the other hand, we can consider an animal like the bald eagle, which owns a span of territory and for the most part lives an isolated life, which also appeals to some people.

Neither model applies to humans: we do not naturally isolate ourselves, like eagles, and we do not naturally dissolve our sense of self in an ant colony or a beehive. Some people take drugs or other inducements to trigger this loss of self, but this is the opposite of what rational people seek in a community. One of the most important points of *The Political Spectrum* was the claim society is not an institution and is therefore not a social organism, which I will address in more detail in the chapter on liberty. What I mean by this for now is although humans naturally form communities that make demands on us, such as resource management and procreation, humans are also ends in themselves and cannot be expected to sacrifice their lives for the sake of the community without a reasonable say in the matter. Ants and bees are not ends in themselves within their communities. Granted, some people will sacrifice themselves for the community, as in the case of war, but this should be a conscious decision in which the person does it for the family and friends he leaves behind. If a state has the authority to dispense with citizens by fiat, we will find ourselves lost with the narrow path nowhere in sight.

In the case of humans, we establish communities to support our emotional and rational interests; notably, to help us achieve our teleological potential to live happy and fulfilling lives. Assuming we structure society in an optimal way, we will establish a means for people to achieve their potential, to fulfill their teleology, while at the same time recognize that the community will make demands on us to keep the community running. As is often said, we cannot talk about rights if we do not first talk about responsibility. The significance of this point is society is not an institution or a social organism that possesses a mysterious existence unto itself with a claim to our blind loyalty in the same way an ant colony or beehive seems to operate with a mind of its own. Likewise with the state or government: it is not a metaphysical entity; it exists within a society to serve the needs of the citizens, even though many states or governments today or throughout history do not have the consent of the people.

The state is a collection of institutions (military, police, courts, education, health, and so on) the citizens establish to keep us safe and provide an environment for us to live happy and fulfilling lives. There is no doubt the state should have the authority to coerce people to behave or not behave in certain ways—a state is generally understood as having a monopoly on legitimate violence within a defined territory—but only after the elected representatives of the people decide which ways the state will have the authority to coerce people to act. As noted in the previous section, I will defer to empirical evidence to decide which institutions a particular society will need to protect people and create an environment in which people are free to fulfill their teleology, but this is the easy part, just as deciding what people need in terms of diet, exercise, and education is the easy part. The more difficult and more important challenge—the true realm of political philosophy—is determining what we need to do collectively to ensure enough wealth and resources are being produced to make society and the modern state possible. Anyone can talk about the need for children to have good schools, but serious individuals consider the realities of human nature and the system of laws and incentives that will be required to produce the wealth and resources necessary to fund the schools.

REFINEMENT

One of the best ways to understand human teleology is to look for the things in life that naturally resonate with us, figuratively or literally. On the figurative level, the wedding scene at the end of romantic comedies resonates with audiences around the world who are often moved to tears. As we watch the man and woman battle back and forth and finally find a way to make love work, something within us resonates at a deep level, as if the universe itself has blessed the union. In their love we recognize a yearning within each of us that transcends culture and time. On a literal level, music resonates with us and evokes emotions and memories. Whether electronic dance music or rock 'n' roll, audiences around the world sing, dance, and devour music throughout the day. I am always amazed by how hearing music from my high school or college years evokes memories and feelings from those times. The list could go on (consider how people respond to beauty, athletic ability, artistic ability, compassion, or hints of the divine), but I have no intention of providing a comprehensive list of what naturally resonates with us. When we are faced with something beautiful or sublime, it takes our breath away as we imagine our own potential and the mysteries of life. We learn something about what it means to be human. If we look at the things in life that resonate with people, often throughout time and across cultures, we can find clues about what it means to be human. Just as plants naturally turn toward sunlight, humans naturally turn toward certain things or patterns of behavior that give us clues about human teleology.

Although what I said might sound like a truism or beyond dispute, there have been thinkers throughout history who deny it, a school of thought called materialism, which often goes hand in hand with nominalism. According to these thinkers, our inner world reflects the material circumstances we live in, not the other way. Rather than take the approach of teleology proposed in this book, in which human nature is real and is revealed in how we structure our societies to help us actualize our real potential, the materialist argues our material circumstances determine our consciousness and inner world experiences. For example, if a society has traditional gender roles, the materialist argues, it is because the material circumstances, not our biology, combined with things like male domination, has shaped us to promote this behavior. This in turn means these same traditional gender roles can be unlearned if we change our material environment. The question is, does the biology of gender naturally give rise to certain gender roles, or are gender roles a complete accident of our material circumstances?

If we limit this point to the claim that our material circumstances influence or shape consciousness, I could not agree more. The inner world or consciousness of a child who is raised in a traditional, middle-class family in a safe home with a good school will differ from the inner world or consciousness of a child who is raised in a broken home in a poor neighborhood with a bad school. However, the fact that materialists place value judgments on these two scenarios is evidence that teleology is real and that relativism is an untenable position. If humans have no teleology and we are nothing more than blank slates that inscribed by our material circumstances, there is no basis to prefer one scenario to the other aside from desire. The only reason for wanting children to avoid broken homes, poverty, and bad schools is they are not positive for our organic growth and maturity, that is, our teleology. Part of the confusion stems from a failure to understand the idea of actual versus potential, which brings us to the next point.

There are many things in life that resonate with people across generations and cultures, but there are also qualitative differences in what resonates with different people and different cultures— refinement. Pop music resonates with some people and classical music resonates with other people, whereas black velvet paintings resonate with some people and sculptures from Ancient Greece resonate with other people. I am not claiming that people who like classical music are superior or are incapable of liking pop music, because both types of music can resonate with the same people on different levels, but we can argue there are qualitative differences or levels of refinement in the things that resonate with us, for two reasons. First, people of different ages resonate with different things due to differences in their biological growth and maturity, evidenced by how cartoons and children's movies resonate with children but not with adults. Adults can be entertained by programming for children, and the best children's stories include subtext for adults, but the material is designed with children in mind—the complexity, the language, the thematic content, and so on. Just as children have to learn to play chopsticks on the piano before advancing to Chopin, the best way to help people grow and mature is to keep them resonating with positive influences that are appropriate for their age. We should not rush children to grow up any more than we should hit the brakes to slow them down, which is why movies and music have rating systems. Second, there are qualitative differences between people of the same age. For example, the comic section of the Sunday newspaper is less refined than *Lolita* or *Robinson Crusoe*, just as operating a cash register is less refined than performing brain surgery.

Getting to the heart of the matter, given that we are organic creatures who grow and mature over time, we can talk about the bell curve distribution of refinement for a particular person or society. (For the record, I use the term "bell curve" as a heuristic to explain my point. I have no evidence to suggest the data are normally distributed, but most people can imagine a bell curve and what bell curve thinking entails.) Our ability to actualize our potential is a function of different variables—natural talent, diet, exercise, training, education, family, luck, competition, and so on. Every year, millions of children join the pipeline to play professional sports but only a small number make it all the way. If hard work were sufficient, more people would rise to the level of professional performance in sports, but this is not the case. The same goes for other careers that tend to pay well for people at the top of their game—actors, singers, writers, doctors, lawyers, and so on.

Throughout society people are working hard and striving to climb the ladder of success. Some people rise due to natural talent, others through hard work, and others simply inherit a good life from their parents. Likewise, some people fail to rise due to lack of talent, lack of effort, or a bad situation or bad luck that makes progress difficult. I will address the fairness of this dynamic in more detail in the chapter on equality, but for now we will focus on how this game plays out as a matter of fact. Where someone ends up in the social hierarchy depends on effort but it also depends on the supply and demand for particular job skills. A person might meet the minimum requirements to go to medical school, but if there are only 1,000 slots available for school but 2,000 highly qualified applicants who far exceed the minimum requirements, then medical school for this person probably is not in the cards. Those of us who need doctors deserve to have only the best students selected for medical school, with the understanding that a person with excellent academic credentials but a limited capacity for caring and empathy probably would never be a good doctor. Granted, a person who was not accepted this year could apply again the next year—never give up—but many aspiring doctors will never become doctors, which is the case for many professions. Some of the most important choices in life involve aiming where we have the best chance of success.

I am not suggesting personal refinement necessarily correlates to income or social status, but as a general rule people must actualize new levels of refinement of their own potential to climb the social ladder. I am also not suggesting that refinement is something we achieve with evolution, with the goal of producing a superior race of people. On the contrary, humans have not changed much during the past 4,000 years and probably will not change much during the next 4,000 years. The key point is that social progress involves individuals fulfilling their potential, not evolving to new levels of refinement. Given that all people need to pay the bills and we are all dead in the long run, people will eventually settle into the natural bell curve of society and culture, which means their refinement arc will naturally plateau and begin to crystallize within the bell curve, like the jazz drummer who never made it and opens a jazz club. The majority of people will find themselves near the middle of the bell curve and a minority of people will find themselves on either tail. The shape and size of the bell curve can change over time, often over generations, but change is gradual and limited by the collective refinement of the population, which is difficult to change in the short term.

For example, in a country where the average person has a middle-school education and cannot read a newspaper, efforts by international aid donors to invest in and promote modern state institutions will often have limited success, especially in the short term, and often provide elites with the means to increase their power. This kind of change happens from one generation to the next with significant social change. What this means, and this is the key, is that most people will fall short of actualizing their full potential, due to reasons within and outside of their control, and they will seek satisfaction in life from things that resonate with their particular level of refinement. The most refined individuals in a society will often seek out more refined types of activities, like philosophy, literature, or artsy movies, and the less refined individuals will often seek out less refined types of activities, such as gambling, drinking, or watching television, but even the more refined individuals enjoy less refined activities in moderation. The reason for this is that people resonate on different levels at different times. Sometimes we want to see Shakespeare but other times we want to see a horror movie and eat popcorn.

The upshot from this analysis is that we should structure our society and our policies in such a way that people can live happy and fulfilling lives within the sweet spot of the refinement bell curve, while at the same time instilling a culture that promotes people fulfilling their social obligations. This process might tend to crystallize some groups of the population in their space of the bell curve and make social change more difficult, but the alternative to this is a perpetual state of revolution. We might prefer that people dedicate more of their free time to intellectual pursuits and less time on watching reality television or drinking in bars, but it is not fair to place such demands on people, especially when many of the people casting aspersions are misguided about their own level of refinement. For most people, after the workday is over and the children are in bed, even if they have any time, money, or energy left over, the options for meaningful hobbies or entertainment are limited. Just as important, the people who live in the sweet spot of the refinement bell curve tend to have a core set of beliefs and values that have stood the test of time—they work—which usually means untested beliefs and values will be viewed with suspicion. If people see with their own two eyes on a daily basis that certain types of behavior and values are required for people to fulfill their social obligations, we should respect this, especially if the alternative is behavior that results in social entropy. The ruthless push for social progress (keeping in mind that not everyone agrees on what progress entails) should be balanced with the understanding that people have a right to live in peace and by their own standard of happiness.

EVOLUTION

The topic of evolution often enters the political philosophy debate, but usually for the wrong reasons. Evolution is a relevant topic for political philosophy and our analysis of teleology, which is why I included it in this chapter, but we should get some wrongheaded ideas out of the way before shifting to our analysis.

Some people highlight the theory of evolution as a veiled or even open way to deny the existence of God, even claiming the theory of evolution and God are incompatible. According to this logic, if we can devise a theory to account for the direction and complexity of evolution without invoking the deity, then we have successfully demonstrated the deity does not exist. This claim might be true, but more evidence and analysis would be required to substantiate it. The logical error of the argument is obvious, however. For example, just because I can account for the wet streets outside by claiming it rained the night before, the streets might be wet because someone opened the fire hydrant. The same error from a religious person would look like this: because I can account for the direction and complexity of evolution by invoking the deity, the deity must exist. Again, this claim might be true, but it requires more evidence and analysis, such as showing it is mathematically impossible for random genetic mutations to account for the biological complexity we see in the world today. The theory of evolution is often said to be grounded on "the survival of the fittest," but this relates to breeding, not evolution. Organisms with strong traits will pass them on to their progeny, with or without evolution. The theory of evolution is ultimately grounded on the claim that genetic mutations are random but can result in the transformation of simple organisms into complex organisms over time.

With the religious right, we often see people deny the theory of evolution because, from their perspective, it conflicts with a Biblical view of the world. As should be clear, however, the Book of Genesis says God created the world in a way that is somewhat consistent with science (plants before animals before humans) and the Big Bang theory (creation from nothing). The most important point for these evolution narratives on the left and the right is that the truth or falsity of the theory of evolution has no necessary implications for the existence or nonexistence of God. The complexity of the universe can be used as a basis to argue for the existence of God, but the theory of evolution by itself provides no basis to argue against the existence of God because God could have created a universe that evolves. This confusion suggests evolution is often raised in the context of political philosophy, on both sides of the political spectrum, for political rather than scientific reasons. Of interest, Michio Kaku, the co-inventor of String Field Theory, concluded that we live in a world governed by rules that were created and shaped by a universal intelligence, not by chance.[1] Anthony Flew, who previously defined the agenda for modern atheism, and Francis S. Collins, the head of the Human Genome Project, reached similar conclusions about God, which means belief in the divine is consistent with scientific reasoning. Therefore, the left should drop this argument, if denying the existence of God is the primary objective, and the right should not fear evolution because it can be used as an argument for the existence of God.

---

[1] https://www.youtube.com/watch?v=lvnSQHhEkc0 (Does God Exist?? Michio Kaku Responds!).

Evolution—genetic mutations—is a fact. We can observe genetic mutations by studying DNA and can track them over time. If scientists study genetic mutations and learn from them, we are adding to human knowledge and should embrace it, without leaving the realm of science to speculate about how or why the genetic mutations happen. This claim is not controversial and does not provide us any insights about political philosophy. (The more controversial claims deal with the origin of life and the evolution of one species into another.) As we transition from empirical evolution to the theory of evolution, however, we enter the realm of metaphysics because the fundamental claim of the theory of evolution cannot be proved with empirical evidence, in particular, the claim that genetic mutations are random.

If a den of black bears were to migrate to the arctic, their children and grandchildren would not automatically grow white fur to improve their chances of survival. If the trees in the savannah were to grow taller, the necks of giraffes would not automatically grow longer to improve their chances for survival. Genetic mutations just happen, randomly, in terms of the timing and direction of the mutations. If the bears are not lucky enough to grow white fur in the arctic, they will probably die because their potential prey will see them a mile away. If the giraffes are not lucky enough to grow longer necks, they will probably die because they will be unable to eat the leaves of the trees. The species that are fortunate enough to have good random mutations—mutations that improve the chances of surviving in a particular environment—will improve their chances of survival, and these beneficial mutations will get passed on to the next generation. The important question is whether any single mutation could have a measurable impact on survival. For example, human DNA has been mutating for the past 4,000 years with negligible results in terms of major changes to our physiology. If evolution is slowing down or gelling, this would lend credence to the idea of teleology.

The reader is encouraged to study evolution in more detail, but we should now consider the claim of randomness. Are the genetic mutations of evolution random? If so, what does this mean? The theory of evolution claims that because genetic mutations are not in response to intelligent design or environmental pressure (to avoid Lamarckism and not confuse it with epigenetics), the mutations must therefore be random. This claim might be true, but there is no evidence to support it—and never could be. What would the evidence look like? The claim that genetic mutations are random is an intuition, a leap of faith that goes beyond the evidence and is therefore metaphysical, not scientific. Let us suppose for the sake of argument that evolution is unfolding in such a way that the genetic mutations could be thought of as revealing a deeper pattern. We cannot collect any evidence that will prove evolution is unfolding according to a deeper pattern, just as we cannot prove evolution is random, but the claim that there must be a deeper pattern would allow us to account for the complexity of the universe in ways that do not crumble in the face of mathematics.

For example, it can be shown with mathematical certainty that a monkey will never type one of Shakespeare's 600-character sonnets by randomly smacking keys on a typewriter (1 in 26^{600}). In fact, one billion monkeys smacking random keys at the speed of a modern supercomputer for one billion years would never produce one of Shakespeare's 600-character sonnets, at least not during the 14 billion short years the universe is assessed to have been in existence. A textual example like a sonnet is relevant because the thing that actually mutates in evolution (DNA) is information. When a beak grows longer to allow a bird to eat more bugs, the DNA text is edited and the growth of the beak follows. We can show with mathematical certainty that smacking random keys on a typewriter will never produce functional computer codes or story-length narratives. (This also raises the question of what made the typewriter or the alphabet.) Just as important, even if we begin with a computer code or story, which presumes the work of a rational mind, random edits will never transform the computer code or story into a more complex computer code or story, unless something other than randomness is involved in the editing process. In fact, any true randomness introduced to the editing process would necessarily produce incoherence in the text over time. The challenge is thus explaining how random edits to the text of DNA can produce greater complexity.

To continue our analysis of randomness, we should consider what random means because the theory of evolution hinges on it. Given that scientific-minded people think of the universe as being governed by laws of nature or causality—we can talk about the uniformity of nature—what does it mean to say genetic mutations are random? If I roll a six-sided die, I have a 1 in 6 chance of rolling a particular number. To have this kind of randomness, however, a rational mind has to design a fair six-sided die, meaning the odds of rolling any particular number is 1 in 6. Next, I have to roll the die because it will not roll itself. Is this what it means to say evolution is random? If it makes sense to talk about the uniformity of nature and every effect has a cause, is there room for randomness in science? (The world of quantum mechanics is often described as random or probabilistic, but we do not live in that world.) If so, this would mean that prior to a particular random genetic mutation, there would be a predetermined list of possible genetic mutations, like the six options on a die. Each of them would have an equal chance of occurring, and then some process, such as rolling the die, would determine which genetic mutation gets selected. Even if we were to accept this concocted scenario, we would still have to account for how the options for genetic mutations were placed on the list and the mechanism by which one was selected.

What we can say with confidence about the theory of evolution, as we return to our analysis of teleology, is it claims life has moved from simple to complex organisms. We can argue about whether the transition from simple to complex organisms was driven by the natural unfolding of deep patterns or by randomness, but the arc of evolution is clear for all to see—simple life gives rise to complex life. In less complex organisms, such as ants or bees, we see no recognition of the individual and submission to the social organism, such that ants and bees blindly give their lives in support of the "greater good." In fact, in the case of ants and bees, the colony or hive could be thought of as an organism that seems to have a mind of its own. In other words, we can view an ant colony or beehive as an institution or social organism because it is directed toward a specific purpose and the individual members are expected to give up freedoms in pursuit of that goal. When this happens in the case of a human society, we call it tyranny or dictatorship.

As we consider more complex species, we see a clear move toward a rise of the individual and away from collectivism and the social organism. For example, with the transition to primates, we begin to see the development of personality and leadership roles within a constructed social hierarchy that are learned and earned based on behavior and with a sense of identity that goes beyond the dictates of birth with defined roles, like drones or a queen bee. Most animals exist in some type of community, but as we focus on the more complex species, we see animals banding together to promote their own individual survival, not merely fulfilling their cog-in-the-wheel functions defined by birth.

If we accept that evolution makes species more complex over time, then the less complex and more primal history of our evolution still has traces in our DNA text. We cannot wipe the slate clean and download an upgrade for human 2.0—our past lingers and reverberates. Somewhere in our DNA remains the more primal tendency to embrace the pre-rational world of collectivism and the social organism, like ants and bees, which in turn means rejecting the rational burden of fulfilling our social obligations to sustain a modern state. This is why overcoming our primal collective tendencies is one of the most difficult obstacles to building a modern state and why all the exit ramps along the narrow path of social progress pointing toward collectivism or the social organism should be ignored. Likewise, we should not be fooled by trendy theories such as Dataism or the Internet of Everything, which run the risk of relieving us of the burden or rational thought and transforming humanity into a giant beehive.

If the universe is evolving in such a way that nothing is eternal, how is it possible to talk about truth? Back to the pre-Socratics we go. Many people on the right, especially the religious right, tend to view the world through the prism of Parmenides, such that the world was created as we see it today and evolution or change is an illusion. Change is not real and the only way to gain truth about the world is to see the timeless being of it all. As such, we should focus more attention on the system as a whole and less attention on the particulars. Whereas, many people on the left, especially materialists, tend to view the world through the prism of Heraclitus, such that the world is in a constant state of change. Only change is real and the only way to gain something resembling truth is to understand the world is in a constant state of flux—truth is relative. As such, the appearance of a cohesive or consistent system is an illusion; particulars are all we have.

As should be clear, the extreme positions of Parmenides and Heraclitus are not tenable and need a solution that universals and teleology can offer. Rather than dig deeper into this important topic, however, I will close with a profound quote with valuable insights about political philosophy and evolution.

> I find it ironic that liberals generally embrace Darwin and reject "intelligent design" as the explanation for design and adaptation in the natural world, but they don't embrace Adam Smith as the explanation for design and adaptation in the economic world. They sometimes prefer the "intelligent design" of socialist economies, which often ends in disaster from a utilitarian point of view.[2]

RENAISSANCE MAN

Most people, whether they know it or not, believe in teleology, at least implicitly, even if they openly reject the term. I challenge anyone to read a book about evolution that does not use words like "purpose" or "design," at least implicitly, while rejecting purpose and design. People on the left and right sides of the political spectrum have a vision for what it means to be a successful or self-actualized human being, and these visions often differ in significant ways. Some people might admire a business mogul because of his success in a competitive

---

[2] Haidt, Jonathan, *The Righteous Mind: Why Good People are Divided by Politics and Religion*, pg. 356.

market or because he creates jobs, whereas other people might frown on him as a selfish person who made lots of money at the expense of others because life is a zero-sum game with a fixed pie. On the other hand, some people might admire a politician who passes a bill to fund a social program to help needy people, but other people might view this as a net drain on society that will take money away from other important programs and make it more difficult to provide funding for needy people down the road. Of course, we cannot pass judgment on a person unless the person is measured against a standard. Why is it is good to be successful in business? Why is it good to fund a social program for the needy? To look at this from the other side, if we want to reserve the right to pass judgment on people who are acting in a way we do not admire or in a way that does not live up to our idea of an ideal person, we have to explain why.

The basic idea of teleology is there is such a thing as human nature that should form the basis of our judgments. We would not admire someone who spins a nice web to catch insects because we are not spiders. We would pass judgment on a woman who eats her mate after having sex because we are not praying mantises. Whether we recognize it or admit it, the only way to praise or pass judgment on another person is to hold them accountable to some standard, and a standard can have no value if it is made up or lacks a foundation. As I have raised previously, the fact that children and adults do not behave the same or that civilized people and people who live in bands or tribes do not behave the same are not sufficient reasons for believing that truth is relative or that there are no objective standards for praising or passing judgment on people. If people are nurtured with proper diet, exercise, and education, natural patterns will reveal themselves during the growth and maturity of the person. Granted, we might suspend judgment on someone if we learn about certain circumstances, such as insanity or abuse, but our ability to suspend judgment makes sense only if there are situations in which passing judgment is justified. If we reflect on our own lives and on our relationships with others, it should be clear that our desires, wants, and ambitions are grounded in the fact that we are biological creatures of a particular nature. It is no accident that men and women on average tend to get married in their mid- to late 20s. It is no accident that we form communities that protect individual rights rather than mirror ant colonies or beehives. If fact, all things being equal, if we know the age and gender of a person, psychology can give us an accurate description of what is motivating the person. Each person is unique, but our behavior patterns through time are consistent and predictable—teleology.

When we think of a Renaissance man, we normally imagine a person with a variety of refined interests—art, music, literature, foreign languages, cuisine, and so on. Obviously, we would not admire or strive to be such a person unless it was possible and somehow integral to our nature at the most refined level. We admire the Renaissance man because he reminds us of our own potential, given the right circumstances. However, to truly admire a Renaissance man, we have to consider more than just the refined talents or tastes he has acquired over time; we also have to consider whether the person has satisfied his social obligations. We might admire a Renaissance man, but we might be less impressed if we discover he is a spoiled brat who is wasting the wealth of his rich parents. Likewise, we might be less impressed if he wanders from one empty relationship to the next in pursuit of sexual gratification and never experiences a mature relationship that results in genuine love. That is, although we all admire the Renaissance man, we should also look at people and society to see the kinds of things people should strive for, both because it is consistent with their nature and because the continued survival of society requires it.

As I alluded to above and as I argued more extensively in *The Political Spectrum*, there are two foundational institutions or truths that we can use as a basis for assessing whether people are satisfying their social obligations. The first institution of resource management led us to the prohibition of deficit spending. If we accept that people within society must be nurtured or cared for during childhood and old age, then we have the right to expect people to be net producers of resources during their adult working years. The second institution of procreation led us to the sanctity of monogamous procreation. If we accept that society has to produce the next generation to survive and that the strongest bond between any two people is between parent and child, then we should promote the traditional family model to ensure children receive the altruistic love they need to grow and mature into adulthood.

The reader will note these two truths are derived solely from analysis of universals. We do not need any worldly experience to know society must produce enough resources and produce the next generation to survive. We know this is true by analysis of universals, just like we know Minneapolis is in the United States. However, as we transition to the specifics of the two principles—notably, the prohibition on deficit spending and the sanctity of monogamous procreation—we have to shift to empirical evidence in the context of human teleology. The same two truths apply to all species that seek outside nourishment and do not self-replicate, but the specifics of how these two principles are accomplished are specific to the species, based on empirical evidence and an assessment of a species' teleology. We know from science that parents naturally give altruistic love to their children and ask nothing in return, which is why we would be foolish to toss this natural altruism aside and raise children in a communal setting by people who do not possess the same level of altruistic love for the children. We also know from mathematics that when a society makes the transition from legitimate debt to deficit spending, some sort of mathematical reset eventually becomes inevitable, usually in the form of a recession or a market collapse. We know this from experience, even if we have ways to delay the inevitable, such as monetary policy. Therefore, to avoid this mathematical disaster, we should implement safety measures to prohibit it from happening in the first place.

In closing, although many people admire the Renaissance man, I would propose that we should also admire the people who are willing to set aside some of their own dreams and desires to satisfy the most fundamental needs of society, while at the same time holding firm to the mantle of liberty that allows them to pursue their own interests and set limits on what society can demand from them. One person might like NASCAR and two-stepping in country bars, which some people might not consider refined, but if he fulfills his social obligations, who are we to pass judgment on how he lives his life? If a person raves about the latest poem he wrote or the latest foreign film he saw, we should admire his quest to expand his horizons and pursue higher degrees of refinement, but if he leaches off his friends and leaves his pregnant girlfriend alone without money, then we have every right to pass judgment on this person. I personally would like to see more people show more interest in more refined activities like art and philosophy, because I have derived so much pleasure from them, but if such a shift within society would result in people doing it at the expense of satisfying their social obligations, like balancing their checking accounts and raising their families, I would say have a sit-down dinner with the family and watch a funny movie with popcorn.

CONCLUSION

We have reached the end of part one (telescope) with our analysis of universals and teleology. If my analysis was successful, it should be clear the two ideas are related, have an important place in political philosophy, and would benefit from additional analysis, which I will do in part two (microscope) by considering universals and teleology in the context of culture, private property, equality, and liberty. This methodology is similar to what I did in *The Political Spectrum*, but I hope I have introduced enough new topics to minimize any overlap or duplication of effort. Just as we can admire a gem by rotating our wrist to see other facets, we can study political philosophy by rotating our wrist to see it though different foundational ideas. As we continue our analysis and gain new insights, my hope is that a faint line will begin to appear on our map as we consider ways to continue along the narrow path of social progress.

PART II. THE MICROSCOPE

CHAPTER THREE. CULTURE

With the survey of universals and teleology behind us, we can now address some important topics of political philosophy through these two lenses, just as we addressed important topics of political philosophy through the two lenses of resource management and procreation in *The Political Spectrum*. If we accept that we often have to go beyond human perception to gain knowledge of the world and of ourselves by the use of universals, such as using scientific equipment to measure densities, frequencies, or chemical reactions, often at extremely small or large scales that we cannot perceive with our senses, then we should have a solid understanding of universals before delving into political philosophy. Likewise, if humans are organic creatures that grow and mature in accordance with deep patterns by making a transition from potential to actual, then we should have a solid understanding of teleology before delving into political philosophy. If we cannot articulate our political philosophy in terms of universals and teleology, even if it means rejecting these ideas with a cohesive and consistent argument, there is a good chance we need to clarify and refine our ideas.

One of the points I stressed in the first two chapters was the idea that just because different people or societies have different values or beliefs over time and in different locations does not mean truth is relative. Some societies practiced infanticide or pederasty, but these are morally wrong from a rational perspective that understands universals and teleology; it is not merely a matter of culture or taste. In many situations, one or more people or societies might simply be wrong, and the mere fact that we have a majority opinion for a particular issue is not sufficient for the attainment of truth. There is no debating a matter of taste, to the extent that people as a matter of fact have different tastes, but this does not mean all tastes are equal or should be celebrated.

Whether sampling wine, food, cinema, books, or Buffalo wings, some people have a more refined sense of taste or judgment and can justifiably be said to be right or wrong regarding which things are better, even if we accept that some people might like other things as a matter of fact. Baseball stadium nachos are not good as far as food critics are concerned, but people still enjoy them. Along the same lines, we can discuss culture, which we will define as the beliefs, customs, and patterns of behavior of a particular group of people in a particular time and place. Implicit in this definition is the empirical fact that cultures change from time to time and from place to place. To this extent, culture and political philosophy are inextricably linked, with an important difference: whereas culture addresses what people in a society do as a matter of fact, the window dressing, so to speak, political philosophy looks at the universals underlying a particular culture and looks for way to make positive changes below the surface (the narrow path) that will eventually manifest themselves on the surface of the culture.

Just as we can combine sodium and chloride to make salt, regardless of the properties we perceive in the sodium or the chloride individually, most of the productive work we do in political philosophy happens below the surface, where most of the iceberg resides and can have dramatic consequences once implemented at the visible level of culture. The same goes for teleology: if we understand that we are organic creatures of a particular nature that grow and develop in predictable ways, then how we shape our culture should be with the idea of creating an external environment that is conducive to promoting our biological growth and maturity.

State of Nature

One of the most important and often misused topics in political philosophy is the idea of humans in a state of nature. I say misused because there has been so much ink and blood spilled and so much disagreement, both because most people have gotten it wrong and because it is not always clear how this analysis can be used as a foundation for political philosophy. As I addressed in *The Political Spectrum*, state of nature analysis is or should be empirical, not theoretical, and the social sciences have done a good job of discrediting the pervasive myths of modern philosophy.

Traditionally, philosophical thinkers have made one of two errors in their state of nature analysis. First, some thinkers, like Hobbes, viewed the state of nature as a state of perpetual warfare—the war of all against all. People, left to their own devices, will try to kill and enslave others and will refuse to play by the rules. Therefore, we need a strong state to impose order with an iron fist on these unruly people. Many conservatives and Republicans tend to view the world this way, but tend to prefer limited government, which seems to suggest people are capable of playing by the rules after all. Second, some thinkers, like Rousseau, view the state of nature as an innocent, idyllic place where people live in harmony—the noble savage. People, left to their own devices, will hold hands and sing Kumbaya in perfect harmony. Therefore, in this case, the creation of a state and social institutions corrupts human nature and causes us to commit violence and other atrocities that we would not otherwise commit in a state of nature. Many liberals and progressive Democrats tend to view the world this way, at least in terms of how people live in a state of nature, but tend to prefer an active government with large institutions to intervene in our lives, which seems to suggest people are not capable of achieving their potential without social institutions after all.

As Fukuyama noted, human cultures developed from bands, to tribes, and finally to a state-level societies, and the "war of all against all" and the "noble savage" are both incorrect, at least in terms of defining human nature. The most important finding was people were socially organized from the beginning, long before the rise of the modern state. As long as people have walked the planet, they have organized themselves, which confirms Aristotle's insight that humans are social and political by nature.

Rivers of ink and blood have been spilled over the idea of a social contract, whereby people at some point in history made a conscious decision to form a state, usually in a rational way that involves people voluntarily giving up certain freedoms in exchange for the security and benefits of a modern state. In the case of the United States of America, we had Founding Fathers who drafted a Constitution that has stood the test of time like no other political experiment in history, but we should remember the Founding Fathers came of age in a colony that was a legacy of the British Empire with an existing foundation of ideas from thinkers like Locke that were used in framing the Constitution.

The social contract approach in many ways begs the question because it does not address how the people developed to the point of being rational people who are capable of making such a social contract in the first place. This was one of the most important points made by Hegel. People can achieve their rational potential only within a community or society, which usually includes irrational elements, and something resembling rational thought should be considered a prerequisite for drafting a social contract, at least one that will stand the test of time. As such, we enter a "chicken or egg" conundrum in which social progress depends on new intuitions, insights, or pattern recognition regarding the universals of society. However, our society at any given point lacks sufficient refinement to reveal these universals to us or push us forward by some magical force. As I will address later in this chapter, part of the secret to solving this "chicken or egg" conundrum is human teleology, in that our biological growth and maturity naturally drive us forward and shape how cultures develop.

Rather than dwell on the state of nature or social contracts, we will shift our attention to how universals and teleology shape the debate by focusing on how people exchange goods and services in a state of nature. In such a state, like the band level, people live in an egalitarian manner and do not have private property in the way we understand it. Prior to the development of agriculture or the concept of money or wealth, people wandered the land, living hand to mouth and struggling to survive the forces of nature, which means their lives were mostly devoid of refined rational thought. They were not reflecting on the size of the universe or the meaning of life in ways we might today.

Just as these people would not understand private property or money, and might even find them shocking or offensive, they also would not understand what it means to be homeless. In a small social group in which everyone knows everyone, like a band, all people would be expected to contribute to the group and would be taken care of by the group. If one person is a good hunter, it meant more food for everyone. The band members would be shocked if a good hunter demanded a disproportionate amount of meat or other zero-sum resources at the expense of others in the group, especially if it resulted in someone ending up hungry or homeless. Although life at the band level was mostly nasty, brutish, and short, and few people in a modern state today would want to live this way, the egalitarian part still appeals to some people in an oddly nostalgic way.

Why, some might ask, have we given up this way of living? Why can we not continue to share the wealth so that no one goes hungry or homeless? This is a fair question. Although it is not logically necessary to give up egalitarianism as we continue along the narrow path of social progress, it is necessary, as a matter of fact, and is driven by universals, especially as societies grow in size and complexity. The more important point is that people living in a state of nature are living in an unrefined level of existence that falls short of our full potential or teleology. Just as most people today would argue that people living in abject poverty and without formal education are unable to fulfill their rational potential, the same goes for people living at the band level with egalitarianism. People living in a state of nature have not reached their full potential, which means their culture or the values they live by are not at the highest level of refinement.

The question now becomes, as we employ universals in accordance with our teleology to make personal and social progress possible, how will our culture and values change? To think about this, we should consider two ways in which social progress is made. First, social progress is made possible by population growth. As our population grows, we free up people to specialize their work so that more types of work can be accomplished with more expertise, such as making shelter, weapons, or tools. If everyone is dedicated to foraging for food, it will be difficult for a group or society to progress beyond the band or tribe level. One consequence of population growth is the social bonds and obligations among citizens grow weaker because more people will be complete strangers to each other, and science has proven that the strongest natural bonds between people are driven primarily by genetics. People in a large society might develop a sense of pride in the tribe or the nation, which could promote altruism or love for their fellow citizens, but the idea of sharing all the wealth in a communal way becomes less practical and an unfair burden as individuality and liberty grow and are allowed to blossom within society. However, population growth is not sufficient because some societies that grow larger merely add more subsistence farmers, which in many ways makes social progress more difficult to achieve because there are more mouths to feed.

Second, social progress is made possible by increased complexity—individual, social, and technological. As we find better and more efficient ways to promote personal growth and development, to organize ourselves (state, institutions, and organizations), to provide for our basic needs, and to create new forms of wealth, we will also see recognizable patterns of social development that will be reflected in our culture.

The important take-away from this section is that the so-called "state of nature" represents an unrefined level of social development in which the group or society takes precedence over the individual. Any desire to return to the values of this stage of social development, to include egalitarianism, would represent social regress, not social progress along the narrow path. Social progress moves away from primitive egalitarianism and toward the rise of the individual and liberty. Not only that, from the view of universals and teleology, the values of people in a "state of nature" do not mesh well with a refined, complex society, which is why foreign aid programs in developing countries are so often ineffective. Malnourished children in bad schools do not benefit much from gaining access to the Internet.

Given that social progress is linked to population growth and increased complexity, we need more refined and more complex ways to produce and distribute resources, ways that will depend on the effective use of universals, not on whim or superstition. The old model of a few hunters killing a deer and sharing the meat with the rest of the group will not suffice. As we make social progress, not only will our society change, but the individuals who live in society will change as well, in a predictable way that is consistent with our teleology. Once we reach the fortunate stage of producing people who are able to achieve their rational potential—people who are capable of drafting a social contract—we can begin dismantling the remaining vestiges of the social organism and replace it with a society and state that are focused on helping people achieve their potential, while at the same time holding people accountable for fulfilling their social obligations.

One of the unfortunate consequences of social progress is that some people will be unable to rise to the challenge, for a variety of reasons, and will take steps to tear down the social progress and complexity, driven by a blind desire to return to the perceived bliss of egalitarianism and the social organism. The important point to remember is that social growth and progress necessarily result in people loosening their bonds and obligations to strangers and in people demanding more control over the resources they produce, consume, and distribute, which means a degree of social inequality is a necessary and unavoidable condition of social progress, which means understanding and managing this inequality will be an important part of political philosophy.

DIALECTIC

If we are willing to entertain the possibility that social progress along the narrow path is possible, in the sense of making the transition from a band or social organism to a modern state in which individuals have the possibility of achieving their teleological potential, then we should analyze this process to identify any causal factors or patterns that might allow us to make sense of it. Historians and social scientists throughout the centuries have attempted this feat in a variety of ways and with varying degrees of success, such as trying to explain the collapse of the Roman Empire or the rise of Christianity, but their particular findings will not concern us in this section. Rather, we will analyze the idea of dialectical movement and how it relates to political philosophy. Although dialectical movement is often associated with leftist or revolutionary thinking, my analysis will show this need not be the case.

The idea of dialectic goes back to Ancient Greece, popularized in the dialogs of Plato, which often had Socrates as the main character. These dialogs usually involved two or more characters (often historical personalities) discussing important issues, such as the meaning of justice, to arrive at a clear definition—a universal—that is capable of standing the test of time. The way it works was after one person proposed an idea, another person explained why the idea was insufficient, which led to more back and forth to gain clarity via a process of elimination. The important points are the process is not linear (it goes back and forth with lulls and spurts) and the process itself plays a key role in any progress that is made. As they say, two heads are better then one, and we have all had the pleasurable experience of "solving the world's problems" with friends.

Just as great inventors rely on trial and error and tinkering to make the best inventions, there is something to be said for the power of trial and error or bouncing ideas off other people. We have all had the experience of our good ideas crumbling in the face of legitimate criticism (assuming we have the courage to recognize it), only to generate better ideas. The same thing can be said for learning to play an instrument, learning a foreign language, or learning to play a sport. Others can see our blind spots and help us see things in new ways. In some of Plato's more esoteric passages he talks about dialectic as a way of achieving wisdom after a long process of preparation that includes mathematics. I do not fully understand what Plato meant by this, but it appears to be an intuitive, mystical process involving the Forms or Ideas, resulting in a final, asymptotic climb toward personal transformation and philosophical wisdom as we contemplate and experience a beatific vision of the Good.

The transition to modern dialectic in many ways began with Kant, was brought to its logical conclusion by Hegel, and was taken in a new direction by Marx. If we recall Kant's view of *a priori* knowledge and how the objects of perception conform to the forms of the intellect, not the other way, Kant invoked what he called antinomies to show the contradictions that arise when we attempt to conceive of transcendental reality, the world beyond perception. As an example of an antinomy, on the one hand, we can say the universe has a beginning in time with limited space (thesis), but we can also say the universe has no beginning in time with unlimited space (antithesis). The two positions are contradictory but also both plausible or at least not logically contradictory (although the Big Bang theory suggests the universe had a beginning and that space is finite). Kant never offered a solution (synthesis) to these antinomies because his point was that knowledge of transcendental reality was not possible, but the thesis-antithesis way of thinking is dialectical in nature.

Hegel, on the other hand, who was a student of Kant, was inspired by dialectical thinking and made it a cornerstone of his philosophy. I have struggled with reading and understanding Hegel, but the important point for this book is that Hegel's philosophy was founded on the idea that history and human societies progress in a dialectical way with a predictable, final stage of refinement, which just happened to coincide with Hegel's 19th century Prussia, which the king was probably pleased to hear. According to Hegel, history was the inevitable unfolding of a rational, nonmaterial Spirit. As Hegel said famously, the real is rational and the rational is real. Hegel took the more mundane idea of dialectic, whereby people achieve knowledge via dialog, and projected it onto the evolution of the universe and human history. Given Hegel's focus on process and change, we can see where his philosophy resonates with Heraclitus. There is a kernel of truth in what Hegel said, but I would suggest few people today agree with Hegel's philosophy writ large. Many philosophers I admire admit they struggled to understand what Hegel meant, but there is something intriguing about the idea that we can account for the transition from primitive bands to modern states as part of the inevitable unfolding of the universe.

The next important evolution in dialectical thinking was Marx, a student of Hegel who moved to the left (some Hegelians moved to the right). Marx's major divergence from Hegel was made by "turning Hegel on his head": rather than argue, like Hegel, that a rational, nonmaterial Spirit shaped the dialectical process with a rational purpose in mind, Marx said material circumstances shaped the inner world or spirit of people in a purposeless way—hence, dialectical materialism. Marx and his followers took inspiration from the theory of evolution, which they believed provided a scientific foundation for their materialistic theory, and probably explains why people on the left are so quick to invoke the theory of evolution in debates about political philosophy. Marx would argue humans respond to their material circumstances, and that how the material circumstances shape our economic activities in turn shapes how societies develop, which is true. For example, inland agricultural societies with a particular level of technology tend to take a particular shape, whereas fishing and trading societies on the coast with a particular level of technology tend to take another particular shape. As our material world changes and we introduce new technology, we change the way we live, which in turn changes the way we think. In terms of how societies progress from social organisms to modern states, Marx focused on class conflict, which is a universal with a shaky foundation. Although Marx's ideas merit study and his dialectical history often feels like pounding a round peg into a square hole, he undoubtedly had many great insights that many people today take for granted, even many people who claim to reject his ideas.

To understand why Hegel's and Marx's positions are flawed, we should turn to what I call dialectical teleology. Whereas Hegel looked to a rational, immaterial Spirit to account for social progress and Marx looked to the random evolution of the material world for social progress, I propose we look to universals and teleology to account for how human societies progress over time. Given that humans with rational minds play a key role in shaping how societies progress, we can say, like Hegel, that ideas or minds play a key role in the process, but it seems more reasonable to attribute this to human minds, not the immaterial Spirit of Hegel. Likewise, although our material circumstances shape our inner world, the Marxist position misses the point that we are more than our material inputs. As I will address in chapter seven, our morality is hard-wired with six "receptors" that operate independently of our material circumstances. Our material circumstances can restrain or facilitate the development of these six receptors, which reveal themselves in predictable ways for all people in all places, but these six receptors do not depend on our material circumstances. People are not blank slates.

If we want to understand how societies progress, we should look to universals and human teleology. Because humans have a particular teleology, they will tend to structure their societies in ways that suit their needs and help them fulfill their potential, but they will often find themselves trapped in suboptimal systems, due to they way they think or their material circumstances. Some societies thrive in resource-poor climates, others societies struggle in resource-rich climates, and so on, so our material circumstances at best play a secondary role in the process of social progress when compared to the importance of human teleology.

Another problem with Marxism is it does not account for the deep patterns of social development around the world and throughout time. If Marx was right that our material circumstances are paramount, then social progress would hinge on material changes, to include diet, which vary significantly around the world. However, history shows that societies have developed in predictable patterns. Of interest, Marxists often speak as if history is inevitable, not random, and naturally leads to a better way of living that they believe is consistent with our nature, which suggests that teleology is more important than material circumstances. It is hard to see how a word like "alienation" could have meaning without teleology—alienation from what? We should manage our material circumstances wisely, for sure, but only so human teleology is allowed to flourish. With dialectical teleology, on the other hand, we have a dialectical process whereby as we achieve higher levels of refinement along the narrow path, we adjust our society to reflect those changes; and as we make changes to society, we create an environment in which we are able to achieve new levels of personal and social refinement along the narrow path, which is a virtuous circle. To use a computer analogy, as we add more hardware, memory, and drives to a computer, it allows us to run more preloaded software programs, which allows us to make more complex calculations and plans.

This virtuous circle of progress is difficult and fragile, but as progress is made, the changes crystallize in our organism and get woven into our social fabric, just as an athlete who trains over the years is pushed to new levels of performance and refinement that become part of his muscle memory. Granted, society is often "sticky," such that we often get stuck in our ways or hang on to traditions beyond their useful life, but there are limits to progress, just as there are limits to what people can do physically or intellectually.

For people to grow and mature in accordance with their teleology, they have to work hard and grind themselves to new levels of refinement each step of the way along the narrow path, and every generation has to do it anew. A doctor cannot pass his wisdom to his son via osmosis; if the son wants to be a doctor, he has to traverse the same rigorous training program. Just as Kant asked us to look at a common phenomenon in an original way (Does the mind conform to the objects of reality or do the objects of reality conform to the mind?), rather than look at how humans conform to the material world, we should look at how humans shape the material world to conform to their needs as rational animals. If we have the good fortune of being born into a modern state, we can accelerate our path of personal refinement with lessons learned from the past, which gives us an advantage over others, but we have to guard against riding the coattails of our ancestors and sliding down the exit ramp of social entropy. In the case of the United States of America, we seem to be following our own dialectical process, with Reagan/Bush (R), Clinton (D), Bush (R), Obama (D), and now Trump (R), which suggests we are still seeking the rational middle.

UNIVERSAL OPPRESSION

At the beginning of this chapter I suggested culture is like window dressing, the activity and behavior we see on the surface, as opposed to the deep meaning or pattern below the surface. Although culture is a technical term for academics and social scientists, average people use the term in a variety of ways to describe the ways people in other countries behave. For example, when I was a young first lieutenant in the U.S. Air Force in Panama, I attended a cultural show with Panamanian men and women dressed in traditional attire performing a traditional dance. In some of the dances, the women put their beauty on display and the men competed for their affections, often with subtle tension until the individual women surrendered to the individual men and they danced together, symbolic of starting their lives together. I imagine different cultures around the world have similar dances that might vary in their presentation or window dressing but all are about the same thing below the surface—the mating ritual of men and women and the miracle of life. The dance in Panama was a beautiful example of celebrating how nature pairs husband and wife to reproduce and raise the next generation. On the one hand, marriage and procreation is a social institution and a social obligation, to the extent the dance is done within a community and we have to produce the next generation to survive as a society, to return the favor our parents did for us. On the other hand, there is an element of free choice and self-fulfillment such that we shape and define our own destiny. This dance was not leading up to a shotgun or arranged wedding.

The important point about this example is it shows the distinction between culture and universals. If culture is what happens above the surface, the window dressing flapping gently in the breeze, universals are the deep pattern or meaning about what is happening below the surface and can be compared from one culture to another, regardless of language, location, or time. All cultures have different ways of ritualizing the mating dance, but at the end of the day they are all aimed at the same purpose: men and women uniting to produce children and help them grow into responsible adults to repeat the process. Therefore, when we compare cultures in the context of political philosophy, we should consider human behavior in terms of universals and teleology, not in terms of culture. For example, in some cultures marriages are arranged, in other cultures the two people getting married make the decision on their own, and other cultures are somewhere in-between, with family and friends both playing role in the process. Therefore, rather than look at the window dressing of a particular marriage ceremony (guests, symbols, rituals, vows, meals, receptions, etc.), we should look to what is fundamental when comparing them. On the one hand, most people in modern states would cringe at the idea of an arranged marriage in which the needs of a family, tribe, or society trump the needs of the individuals in terms of having children and staying married, even though there is something to be said for family or society weighing in on such an important decision. Given the high divorce rates we see today, which is due primarily to the ease of getting divorced without social stigma, there is something to be said for the idea that allowing young people to marry whomever they want has not worked out so well.

To speak objectively about a social institution like marriage, we should understand why it exists, or the variables that would make marriage cease to exist in the absence of these variables. As many philosophers throughout history have recognized, the union of man and woman for the purpose of procreation is the fundamental institution of any society, such that all social order and progress depends on getting this institution right to make social progress on the narrow path, with the understanding that we can never "transcend" this social institution. We can establish this *a priori* by taking into consideration the biological fact of the two genders and the mathematical fact of the need for each couple to produce at least two children to sustain the population. The natural altruistic bonds within the traditional family structure hold society together and cannot be replicated outside of this family structure.

Once we understand the *a priori* truth of procreation, we can then talk about what kind of window dressing we will use to implement this social institution for our particular culture, which will depend on our circumstances and history. The important point is the universals provide the foundation for the window dressing, not the other way. The more we understand and accept this truth, the more we realize and accept that our own individual needs, desires, and wants are of secondary importance. As luck would have it, however, for most people who submit to the *a priori* truth of procreation, this will be their primary source of happiness and fulfillment in life.

In the history of Western civilization, one of the most significant changes was the transition from Paganism to Christianity. On the surface, the transition from making offerings at the temple of Venus to worshiping at a Christian church could not be more different. However, if we look below the surface, the transition was not as dramatic as it appeared, such as a general belief in the divine, which is why the transition was gradual and eventually widely accepted. For ancient populations accustomed to the idea of a suffering deity who died and was resurrected (Osiris, Dionysius, etc.), the story of a living, breathing man named Jesus already resonated with people on a deep level and did not demand a dramatic shift in their core beliefs or universals. A Christian, of course, would argue these resurrection myths (Osiris, Dionysius, etc.) were foreshadowing of actual things to come in history.

On the other hand, if we turn to international aid programs in developing countries, the programs often fail because the societies have not developed to the right size or complexity to absorb the programs. You can build a modern factory but it will not function if there are no skilled workers. In many cases, these aid programs perpetuate poverty because the elites steal the money and use the programs to perpetuate their grip on power, which often includes not spending money on social programs like public education or health. It should surprise no one that tribal leaders in Afghanistan are not chomping at the bit for democracy.

The key point of these two examples is we have to distinguish culture or window dressing from the underlying universals that give culture its foundation. For democracy, the mere fact that a particular population holds elections does not tell us much about the kind of culture they have. Some governments allow only one party to run; other countries are so corrupt that the voting results do not reflect the will of the voters; and other countries have powerful political parties that unfairly influence the democratic process. Democracy is more than casting ballots. If we want to understand what is happening in a country, we have to dig a few layers deeper: who controls access to running for office, who controls appointments to senior government positions, who controls the budget and money supply, and so on, which we can discuss regardless of culture.

Shifting to a topic getting attention these days, what does it mean to complain about Dead White Men? Every mature culture should reflect honestly on its past, recognize any mistakes that were made, and avoid repeating the same mistakes, but we seem to have reached the point of needless self-flagellation. When I was growing up, we spoke about the Founding Fathers with reverence, but now many people seem ashamed of them and dwell on the fact that some of them owned slaves, ignoring the more important fact that they created the greatest constitution in history and that it changed the world as we know it, which launched a wave of freedom around the world that liberated nations and freed slaves. Not only that, the tradition of studying Dead White Men as the foundation of a liberal arts education is now under attack or categorized as white male oppression.

A pragmatic approach to this *faux* problem would be to recognize that most of the greatest of works of art, philosophy, science, and literature in Western civilization were, as a matter of fact, done by Dead White Men, but then take steps today to ensure we encourage all people to do their best from this day forward. That is, we can recognize that some Dead White Men might have benefited from privilege, in terms of the positions they obtained within society, but we can also recognize their works were great, have stood the test of time, and should remain at the core of a liberal arts education. There were many people who were not white men who probably could have produced great works if they had been given the opportunity, but most of them were not given the opportunity and most of them did not produce great works, however unfortunate that might be. Rather than dwell on the superficial aspects of race and gender, we should focus on the merits of the great works. Just as we are instructed to not judge people today based on race, gender, or other categories, we should not judge the greatest works of Western civilization just because they were made by Dead White Men.

The key issue for this section is universals are blind to superficial traits like race, gender, or the window dressing of culture. Dead White Men might have had some control over which universals shaped society over the centuries, but they did not own them. Universals are true for all people. Most important, the universals were effective and helped us recover from the collapse of the Roman Empire and rise up with modern states. Many Dead White Men committed horrible acts in history, just as all groups throughout history have, but we can at least salvage the great work they did with valid universals without throwing out the baby with the bath water.

When we consider the challenges we face today, we should look below the surface, for universals rather than on the surface of window dressing. Oppression exists, but only on the superficial level of window dressing, not on the deeper level of invalid universals. Valid universals cannot be oppressive, any more than we can be oppressed by the truth. We might not like the truth, but that is our problem. When people enslave people or deny their rights, they are not doing so based on valid universals—on the contrary. If we expect people to work before paying them, we are not oppressing them. If we expect students go to school and do their homework, we are not oppressing them. If we expect people to live within their means, we are not oppressing them. Living up to the demands of universals is demanding and challenging, which is why the path of social progress is narrow.

Although it might feel oppressive at first to be subjected to the demands of universals, such as learning a new skill, the universals will eventually work their way into the fiber of our existence and shape the way we behave and perform over time. The most capable artists are good at hiding the grueling journey that brought them to their level of mastery. A single brilliant brush stroke can embody thousands of hours of practice and years of apprenticeship under the masters. According to some studies, it takes about 10,000 hours for someone with sufficient natural talent to achieve mastery in a particular skill, which inevitably involves the use of universals until they become second nature. Just as parents use universals to keep their children on the narrow path, any society that takes steps to do the same for its citizens is a caring society, not an oppressive society.

MULTICULTURALISM

One of the most misused and misunderstood terms shaping the political debate today is multiculturalism. As a general rule, people on the right are not fond of the term except in the generic sense of respecting the right of people to live how they choose to as long as they do not violate the rights of others. Many people on the left, however, seem to have made multiculturalism an oblique way to achieve a political objective. Like many abstract concepts, we should analyze the building blocks of multiculturalism before passing judgment one way or another.

If we recall dialectic and consider that societies change and develop over time, in response to variables internal and external to the people living in those societies, there is something to be said for the idea of different cultures coming together, exchanging ideas, and finding ways to survive and thrive through a process of trial and error. Just as we can benefit from discussing a topic from different perspectives to reach solutions via dialectic, the same can be said for different cultures having a culture dialog to find out what works via trial and error. Just as DNA tends to weaken over generations in a scenario of limited genetic variety, such as a tribal culture that ops for marriage within the tribe, societies can stagnate over time they fail to pursue the equivalent of genetic variation. Two heads are better than one, no one has a monopoly on the truth, and so on. On the surface, the idea that culture benefits from outside influences such as other cultures (multiculturalism), seems to be true. In the case of the United States of America, we have had waves of legal immigrants from around the world, and there is no doubt that all of these groups have contributed to the American miracle. On this point, most Americans on the left and the right seem to have reached consensus. Like most abstract and complex issues, we have to dig deeper and split more hairs before getting to the core of the issue, to identify the key universals below the surface.

When we consider multiculturalism, we should remember it is limited by human teleology. When we talk about laws, education, and welfare, we should remember we are mortal, organic creatures with a specific nature. We cannot understand universals without considering teleology, just as we cannot understand teleology without considering universals. For example, if we know economic progress depends on people risking their wealth to create positive cash flow assets or businesses (universals), and that people by nature are risk-averse (teleology), then society should provide incentives for people to take risks with their wealth. Most people would not do it on their own, left to their own devices, especially if taxation is burdensome, bankruptcy laws do not exist, or we have a culture that attacks rather than celebrates success. Instead, people will wait for others to risk their own money or create jobs, which might never happen. What this means is the fortunate people who happen to be successful in business (most businesses fail) will probably be wealthy relative to others. However, without the right incentive, few people would risk their wealth on business ventures.

Therefore, whereas cultures benefit from outside influences to keep them looking for new ways to do things better, core human needs are limited and lead us down a narrow path to recognize some ways of living are better than others, especially within a defined area. If we consider that most people have limited disposable income after they have paid for their rent, cars, utilities, and groceries, then most of the work we do in life will revolve around satisfying these basic needs. And if we consider that most of these basic needs can be reduced to mathematics via balancing the checkbook, then culture within a bell curve distribution of refinement is more limited than most people imagine.

When we consider culture, we also have to consider the difference between culture at a superficial level and universals at the deeper level. For example, people with a limited understanding of Mexican history or culture might celebrate Cinco de Mayo at a local watering hole. Most people enjoy the opportunity to explore other cultures on a superficial level, such as Saint Patrick's Day, a hookah bar, Thai food, or Flamenco dancing. Variety is the spice of life. On a deeper level, a couple might choose to have a Native American holy man perform their wedding ceremony. Most societies can survive this type of multiculturalism that is superficial or limited in nature. This happens every day and in every state. In fact, liberty demands that people be allowed to do many things without government interference. However, when these superficial instances of multiculturalism work their way down to the roots that hold a particular society together in a cohesive and consistent way, the consequences are less innocent.

From a social conservative perspective (more on this in chapter seven), multiculturalism is viewed as an attempt by the left to gratuitously or unwittingly shake up the core values that hold society together. The concern is that the left is so focused on the idea that our society is an unfair power structure inherited from Dead White Men that they do not take the time to honestly assess whether the idea of multiculturalism is sound or effective. Culture and institutions develop over time and are not the product of a cabal of Dead White Men. The march of history has been a long, dialectical process in which trial and error showed us what does and what does not work, and we should be more circumspect about the notion that we can simply uproot our culture or institutions that developed over hundreds or thousands of years. Individual liberty and freedom are important, but they will be short-lived if we neglect the heavy lifting of social responsibility that makes them possible.

This dialectical process is limited by our teleology and the real world, such that we can reach the end of the process for some areas of life. I cannot imagine a world in which broken homes would help children grow up to be responsible adults. I also cannot imagine a world in which deficit spending without regard for mathematics would help people or society accumulate wealth and plan for retirement. Fukuyama first raised the idea of "The end of history," which seems to be true in certain aspects of our life and in the context of teleology: reaching the end of history is the point where most of our potential is actualized, or the point where incremental gains are cost prohibitive. For people who have realistic expectations about life, this is not surprising, but for people who believe in perpetual progress or Utopia, the idea of focusing our efforts on mundane problems or maintaining the status quo might seem depressing.

One of the biggest challenges of living in a modern state with a cohesive and consistent system of universals is that universals are demanding. The free lunch option is not real. If a society accepts that wealth must be created with risky investments before it is distributed, and then weaves this principle into the fabric of society, then those who do not take risks and depend for their livelihood on those who do will probably have a lower income than those who took risks and succeeded, assuming we aspire to live in a modern state democracy with tens or hundreds of millions of people. Given how frequently businesses fail, it is better for private citizens to risk their own wealth rather than for the government risk our tax dollars, often in response to political pressure, as this transfer of risk from society to the individual will result in more prudent decisions. Society should take steps to manage inequality with laws and taxes, but never to the point of stifling the incentive to take risks to create wealth. Humans by nature are risk-averse and need incentives to risk their wealth, especially when we consider that most businesses fail. The key point is that any argument for multiculturalism should be premised on the idea that it strengthens our universals and our prosperity, with the understanding that not all forms of culture will work or should be embraced.

CIVIL SOCIETY

A culture is a complex network of individuals, organizations, and institutions where people manifest various patterns of behavior. Throughout history, it has been popular and fruitful to talk about civil society, which we will define as the non-governmental institutions and organizations that exist in society for the citizens. From the perspective of political philosophy, civil society is important for two reasons. First, the existence and persistence of civil society tells us something important about human nature and the proper ends of society. Humans are ends unto themselves and cannot be subjected to the whims of the state, which means there should be a space within society largely outside the reach of the state and that the state exists to protect. Second, by understanding what civil society is, it helps us understand the other components of society, which in turn shapes the political philosophy debate. Once we understand that the state should limit its interference in civil society, as long as the laws are being obeyed and people are behaving in accordance with liberty, we can rule out certain forms of government.

The best way to begin the discussion is with an analysis of the institutions that are not part of civil society or the government. For simplicity, we will define this type of institution as a collection of individuals working together for the accomplishment of a particular goal, often when money is on the line. For example, a professional sports team is an institution that recruits players to win games and championships. Sports fans can be thought of as part of civil society, but not the cash flow reality of running the sports team. A company is an institution that recruits employees to sell products or services. The important point is this type of institution has a goal that transcends the interests of the individual members and often requires them to do things that go against the grain. Granted, the members benefit from these institutions (money, job satisfaction, social status, etc.), but the goal of the institution (championship, profits, etc.) is of primary importance for institutional survival. A professional sports team that loses every game and loses its fans will cease to exist, just as a business that fails to sell any products or services will cease to exist. We have institutions like this because collective behavior, subjected to the forces of creative destruction, usually outperforms the work of individuals—the whole is greater than the sum of the parts. Much of our social progress depends on these institutions because they are often the primary source of wealth creation.

One of the realities of institutions that aspire to this type of success is that they should be free to select and eliminate members, like varsity football teams or an S&P 500 company, with the goal of improving the overall performance of the institution. If an institution is to succeed, which often means optimizing individual and team performance, the institution has to recruit and train the right individuals to help the institution achieve its goals, such as winning a championship or selling more products. Many institutions are not ruthless or cutthroat (rightly so, thank goodness) and for pragmatic reasons will not eliminate employees on a whim, because this type of behavior often breeds discontent for all the players or employees. However, for institutions to function properly and for society to benefit from these institutions, the goals of these institutions should have the priority. If less talented people are hired or the standards are lowered, performance will decline, the institution will suffer, and society will benefit less.

One of the important arguments in this book is that society is not an institution or social organism, like a professional sports team or business, and now the reason should be clear. First, no one wants to live in a society that actively recruits new members (foreigners) and kicks out poor performing existing members (citizens) in the name of efficiency or progress, which means society by definition is not and cannot be an institution. The whole point of a society is that it is something we belong to, by birth or by naturalization, warts and all, with the cards were dealt. We have a right to expect certain things from society in exchange for satisfying our social obligations and playing by the rules, even if it means some segments of society will bog us down with various inefficiencies. Our society might have expectations for us or judge us one way or the other, but expulsion does not exist in modern states—prison or homelessness, perhaps, but not expulsion, which is one of the defining elements of institutions.

Second, given that society is not allowed to add or remove members at will, it would be incorrect to think about society as an institution in the same way that a professional sports team or an S&P 500 company is an institution. Society can have goals, such as promoting fairness and safety for all citizens, but society does not and should not have any specific goals to which all citizens should be required to pursue or contribute. Society provides a space for us to fulfill our own teleology and live happy and fulfilling lives. We are ends unto ourselves and the state is a means to an end. Reflecting on the idea of a social organism, such as an ant colony, beehive, or dictatorship, a social organism differs from human society in the sense that a social organism is an institution, meaning all the members are expected to contribute to the goal of the institution, even at their own expense, evidenced by how ants, bees, and peasants are expected to blindly give their lives to the greater good. In a social organism, individuals are not free to opt out of the "greater good" or pursue their own path their own way, which is precisely what it means to live as a free human being.

In addition, we should also consider organizations, which we will define as other informal social groups that serve other human needs, to include satisfying our desire for membership or making our society a better place to live. This does not mean organizations will not enjoy some friendly competition or push us to do better, such as a chess club, but in many ways, membership is an end in itself. These organizations are completely voluntary in terms of whether a person chooses to join, but they are not necessarily open to everyone. Just as people are free to express their interest in joining an organization, the organization is also free to decide who joins. If liberty and fairness are to have any meaning, it must also include freedom of association. The problems begin when these organizations are viewed as an extension of the state or when the state views these organizations as a threat. Some examples of organizations include churches, professional associations, or sports clubs. After people have finished working to pay the bills, usually by working at an institution, and after people have paid their dues to society, organizations are where we seek meaning and fulfillment in a way that is unique to us, on our own terms. Whether we are playing darts on Tuesday night with our friends, worshipping on Sunday, or planning a county fair, these are all productive activities that give our lives meaning and make society better. It is in this realm, apart from the state and apart from the wealth-creating institutions, where we find civil society.

For a modern state to survive and thrive, it requires a robust civil society because it is a critical part of the social dialectic (learning by trial and error) that helps us establish patterns of behavior (culture) that will stand the test of time. The state cannot impose social values in a top-down manner that will have a positive, lasting impact. Civil society is where dialectic works its magic to help people find what does and does not work, both in terms of working together and resolving conflicts. The state serves an important role, such as enforcing the laws and protecting people, but people need more than this. They need ways to pursue their own interests or ends without outside interference. The time we have to dedicate to these activities might be limited, but it would be difficult to imagine life without them. If we accept that people are ends unto themselves and that the state is not, it should be axiomatic that the state should have no right to interfere in civil society as long as no laws are being violated and people are behaving in accordance with the spirit of liberty. Life is not always about maximizing profits and obeying laws. We should all have the right to pursue our own ends, to be defined by us, apart from any interests the state or institutions might have.

Conclusion

As the social sciences have made clear, culture matters. Culture made it possible for countries like South Korea and Taiwan to transition from developing country to developed country status in one generation. Culture made it possible for countries like Switzerland and Japan to succeed with limited natural resources. As I proposed is this chapter, culture operates on two levels—the superficial level of window dressing and the deeper level of universals. Although societies are regulated by universals, we should remember that universals are limited by teleology. Unlike Hegel, who claimed a rational, nonmaterial Spirit shaped the development of human history, and unlike Marx, who claimed our material circumstances shaped the development of human history, my proposal in this chapter was human teleology played the key role in shaping the development of human history from subsistence farming to the modern state. As humans find new ways to actualize their potential, by design or by luck, society and culture will change to accommodate this. And as our society makes qualitative changes along the narrow path of social progress, it will be easier for our children to pick up where we left off. I am not suggesting history is automatic or inevitable or that we can know the trajectory of a society in advance (we do not have a map for the narrow path), but if we want to gain insights about how human history develops, we should have a solid understanding of universals and teleology.

CHAPTER FOUR. PRIVATE PROPERTY

Most people living in modern states probably take private property for granted, but it is one of the most important and controversial topics in political philosophy. The logic goes something like this: if I work for money to buy things from others (and they are the rightful owners), then I have the right to consider these things my private property. This probably sounds simple and obvious, but people living at a band or social organism level of existence might find it astounding. They might ask us how private property began in the first place—the gods? royal decree? If we cannot give private property a legitimate foundation, is it legitimate? With private property, no one has a claim to what I bought or inherited, and I can ask the police to pursue criminal charges against anyone who takes my private property without my permission or without fair compensation.

Hume interestingly argued that private property was the foundation of the concept of justice in the sense that the idea of justice would not occur to anyone in a society that lacks private property, such as people living at a band or social organism level of existence. Hume was correct in that it does not make sense to talk about deserving things unless people can be thought of as owning things that others cannot take. In a band or social organism level of existence in which property is shared communally—no one owns anything and everyone has a claim to everything—it is hard to imagine a scenario in which conflicts would arise over ownership, although things like control over sex and power come to mind. If a band hunter kills a deer, the meat will be distributed fairly (not necessarily equally), just as it would within a family. Something resembling justice will always exist, such as one tribe seeking revenge against another tribe for the wrongful death of a member, but Hume's claim that private property was the foundation of justice is interesting and insightful.

Most people in modern states accept the idea of private property but some complain the idea of private property is abused or that private property is distorting relations among humans. For example, it is not inconsistent for someone to embrace the idea of private property and yet be indignant about a person who manipulates the economic or legal system, illegally or immorally, to acquire private property at the expense of others. Some people are offended by the idea that people can inherit private property from their parents, even though these same people would probably demand the right to spend their own money as they see fit if they were to win the lottery.

Even more complicated is the idea of private property as it relates to common goods, such as air or water. Water is a natural resource for all to consume in a state of nature, but as a society grows in population and complexity into modern state, even natural resources like water often have to be brought under the rubric of private property or state control to ensure the resource is managed in a rational way. For example, a government might claim access to a water supply to purify it and distribute it to members of a society in exchange for money, with the goal of promoting good health and preventing diseases. Given how critical fresh water is to life, it should not surprise anyone that we go to great lengths to ensure people have access to clean water and that no one is allowed to exploit it for personal gain, to include artificially lowering the supply to artificially raise the price. The government might even impose restrictions or fines to manage the water supply. On the other hand, a private company might tap into the same sources of water to sell it in plastic bottles at outrageous prices, with quality that is often no better than tap water.

Turning to religion or spirituality, we are often told we should not be obsessed with private property or allow it to control us. Some people say love of money is the root of evil, which has implications for how we understand private property. If we follow the reasoning or logic I have tried to establish in this book, the mere fact that the idea of private property can be abused or that obsessing about private property is not healthy does not contradict the claim that private property is a legitimate universal that is essential and beneficial for life in a modern state.

A RATIONAL MATTER

The fact that most people agree that some things are private property and other things are not private property, depending on the situation, means private property does not exist in a state of nature per se, independent of humans or societies. Private property is a universal because we can predict with great accuracy how the idea develops as society continues along the narrow path of social progress (the rational use of private property keeps us on the narrow path), but we cannot point to an object in the world and say it is necessarily private property, although the complexity or refinement of some objects might suggest they are private property. For example, we can consider the atomic number or density of gold to identify it as a substance, a universal independent of a human mind. Or, we can consider DNA to identify a particular species that is true independent of a human mind. However, we cannot do the same with a plot of land to assess whether someone owns it as private property. What this means is that if rational creatures ceased to exist, so would private property, but this does not mean private property is not a valid universal. If we cannot always identify private property by analyzing something with our senses or other tools, then the logical conclusion is that private property is an abstract universal, similar to how other important ideas in political philosophy are abstract universals, like justice or liberty.

If we look to the animal kingdom, we see hints of private property, such as a squirrel collecting acorns for the winter or a beaver building a dam. There is no doubt these animals would consider these objects their own, to use human language, and would probably attempt to defend or protect these objects from outsiders, but does this mean animals have private property? It does, to the extent that animals act as if they own something and to the extent that animals appear to respect the property of other animals, but it does not to the extent that animals have no recourse and do not understand the idea of private property. In the case of babies, it is clear they desire to possess toys or candy and do not respond well to losing toys or candy, but this does not mean that babies have private property in terms of the baby having a rational understanding of private property.

Locke was famous for saying humans had private property in proportion to the labor or effort they imparted onto an object, such as turning a pile of wood into a house or clearing and plowing a field to grow crops—something that otherwise would not have happened on its own. This point is insightful because people who dedicate their labor or effort to make something better or useful are often thought of as having a claim to it. A squatter, however, could make a similar claim if he cleans up someone's garage to have a place to sleep, so the principle requires some clarification. Locke's labor and effort argument is questionable because one person might randomly buy a stock and sell it the next year for a profit whereas another person might buy the same stock after extensive research (effort) and make the same profit—yet, both have equal claim to the stock and the profit. Likewise, if I by chance buy a piece of land and discover hidden treasure or oil, my increase in wealth and private property will not be correlated to my labor or effort. Marx also tried to link the price of an object to the labor it takes to make it—the labor theory of value—but the same problems apply. Labor has no inherent value—zero. The labor required to make something can help us conduct break-even analysis to assess whether the project is economically viable, but labor cannot dictate the price in the market, and in many cases is irrelevant to determining the market price. If there is no demand for a product or service at a particular price, a fair and honest assessment of the labor required to produce the product or service will not change anything.

As I addressed previously, people living at a band or social organism level of existence do not have private property, at least by our understanding, but this is directly related to the fact that all the goods and services are shared—egalitarianism. If everyone has an equal claim to everything in the group, it does not make sense to introduce the idea of private property or intellectual property. However, as societies grow in size and complexity, as most people become strangers to each other, and as receiving and distributing wealth from a centralized location becomes impossible, then it becomes a practical and mathematical necessity to introduce the idea of private property to keep the game fair and productive.

To clarify this point, consider what would happen if band or social organism rules were to apply in the United States of America. Imagine if anyone at any time could enter your home and take your things without your permission and that you could do the same to other homes. Most people would agree we should take steps to help the needy and prevent people from illegally acquiring things, but no one, with perhaps the exception of the insane or saints, would open their doors for all to partake. Groups of people within a society might form a commune or eliminate private property for the group, which is an option for people in a free society, but once the size and complexity of a society grow beyond a certain point, private property must be introduced and allowed to develop, or our journey along the narrow path of social progress will grind to a halt. Granted, the beginnings of private property will probably be crude and riddled with violence or mysticism, such as granting power to anyone who wields a rod or a sword, but all social progress along the narrow path will depend on society developing the idea of private property in a rational way to absorb the growing size and complexity of the population.

Shifting to teleology, because the development of society should be geared toward creating a social structure that facilitates the growth and maturity of humans in accordance with their nature (teleology) in a sustainable way (each generation pays it forward), we should consider how teleology relates to private property. Just as society requires private property to grow and develop, such that a modern state is not possible without private property, the same goes for humans. To the extent that our most refined achievements, such as art, philosophy, and science, depend of the growing size and complexity of society (we will never find the likes of Bernini, Aristotle, or Newton in a band or social organism), the most refined achievements of humans depend on private property. Granted, a group of artists, philosophers, or scientists might isolate themselves to live in a commune while producing refined works they can sell to support themselves. However, for these artists, philosophers or scientists to have developed their minds and skills to the point of creating these refined achievements, they must have been raised in a society of a minimum size and complexity and they must have isolated themselves from a society of a minimum size and complexity that has a demand for their products. For families to acquire nutritious food for children in a modern state, private property must exist. For a community to collect taxes to build schools for children, private property must exist because you cannot collect taxes if no one owns anything.

One of the great myths of political philosophy is the belief there is no necessary link between the existence of private property and social or technological progress (the narrow path). If we are to believe this myth, it is possible to have all the benefits of a modern state, such as computers, cell phones, or trains in an egalitarian existence without private property. Just as we need specific tools to construct a house, we need private property to construct a growing and complex society, for reasons I will address later in this chapter. The tool (private property) develops over time in a dialectical manner, such as the creation of intellectual property in the more advanced stages of social progress. This means the definition of private property, in terms of what it encompasses, is not static, but the pattern (from potential to actual) has a predictable arc that reflects the needs of human teleology, which is how we avoid the fire of Heraclitus.

The definition of private property develops in an organic way with the development of society. People can pervert the idea of private property into an inflexible absolute, but this does not mean the universal is invalid, which is how we avoid the immovable one of Parmenides. Just as it is a mistake to invoke the social contract theory, because the existence of people who are capable of drafting a social contract are the product of an already refined society, it is also a mistake to suppose that all the benefits of modern states are possible without all tools, such as a rational understanding of private property. As I will address later in the chapter, humans often grow and develop better when they are not subjected to the cold logic of profits and private property, but the fact remains that a modern state must have private property to sustain itself and avoid social entropy.

WEALTH CREATION

One of the most important *a priori* truths in political philosophy is that a society must create wealth before it can be distributed. The proof is to try to imagine a society in which we could distribute wealth that does not exist. Although this might seem so obvious as to not merit our attention, some people do not seem to accept it, or they believe wealth sprouts effortlessly from trees. What this means is they focus on the easy part (telling us what people need to grow and mature in accordance with their teleology) and pay less attention to the more challenging task (creating the wealth that gets distributed). However, we are getting ahead of ourselves. To keep things as simple as possible, wealth is whatever is left over after all the bills are paid. If at the end of the month I have $500 in my checking account and all my debts are paid, then my wealth is $500. On a less abstract level, if I am an apple farmer with a crop of 10,000 apples and I can cover all my bills by selling 8,000 apples, then my wealth is 2,000 apples (which I would be wise to sell as soon as possible to avoid spoilage). However interesting this might be, it raises an important question: do we need private property to create wealth?

The first step is to make an important distinction between wealth and wealth creation. If a wandering band happens upon a plush valley filled with more fruit, berries, and animals than they can eat, they could be thought of as wealthy because they could take the extra food and trade it with other bands for other goods and services. Or, in a country that discovers oil, they could be thought of as wealthy because they could trade the oil with other societies. It takes technology to extract oil, which presumes a certain level of social refinement, but foreign companies could pay fees for the rights to the oil, in which case the country would gain wealth by doing nothing. Mother Nature is by far the greatest producer of wealth, which should not surprise us because most life would cease to exist if Mother Nature did not produce all this wealth. Everything animals need to survive can be found in nature, but can the same be said for humans? All things being equal, it is better to live in a land that is rich in natural resources, but this is no guarantee of economic success, just as having limited natural resources is no guarantee of economic failure.

When we shift to wealth creation, there are two considerations. First, in the creation of "natural" things, such as food, we can use our rational minds to create things in ways that Mother Nature does not, such as tapping into and amplifying the creative power of Mother Nature. For example, in the case of agriculture, we can find an area with good soil, clear out the trees and rocks, plow the soil, and plant seeds with fertilizer to optimize the yield per acre, rather than allow seeds to blow in the wind and settle in the soil randomly. We can rotate the crops and allow fields to remain fallow some years to protect the soil. We can make calculations about how much food to grow. If we know one acre of food will feed 10 percent of the population, we can plant 10 acres to ensure everyone has enough food, or more if we want to trade with our neighbors or plan for unforeseen circumstances. The same goes for hunting. If we know we need 20 pounds of meat for a feast, we will continue hunting until we have 20 pounds of meat; or, more wisely, we will domesticate animals so we always have a steady supply of meat.

Second, in the creation of "unnatural" things, such as cars, skyscrapers, or novels, we use our rational minds to create things that do not sprout effortlessly from the bounty of Mother Nature. Just as it seems odd to me that human hair and fingernails keep growing, which is not the case for other animals, it is telling that we possess the ability to create these "unnatural" objects. In fact, many people point to the creation of these unnatural objects as a criticism of modern states (too much technology and materialism), but this is looking at the situation from the wrong perspective. Rather than think about whether these objects are "natural" in the context of Mother Nature, we should ask whether they are natural in the sense of helping us achieve biological growth and maturity in accordance with our teleology. To the extent that food, shelter, transportation, art, music, books, and other goods facilitate our biological growth and maturity as rational animals, as a means to an end, we can think of them as natural.

So far, this analysis seems straightforward, but we still have to address why wealth creation depends on private property. Although it goes without saying that society and wealth creation depend on Mother Nature and the sun, in this context we are talking about the natural or unnatural wealth creation that depends on the rational mind, through activities like the invention and commercialization of whey protein powder or mini-vans, not the kind of natural wealth creation we find in nature, such as fruit trees or animals. A better question is whether there is anything to prevent an egalitarian society without private property from creating wealth and taking the narrow path to a modern state. The answer to this question is no, in part because people have a tendency to imagine educated and refined people rising to the challenge, but these educated and refined people were the product of a modern state that relied on private property— the same chicken or egg conundrum we have with the social contract theory. To accurately answer this question, we have to set aside our propensity to project our own rational nature onto others and ask whether people living in an unrefined state of nature in which no one has absorbed the benefits of a modern state could make the transition from subsistence farming to creating wealth without private property.

On an emotional level, we know human nature is such that we will naturally claim ownership of certain things as a matter of fact, even if the claim is not legitimate. For anyone who disagrees, I encourage you to observe babies with toys or candy. Also, we know that people who own things are more likely to take care of them, evidenced by how rental neighborhoods are less maintained than neighborhoods where the owners live in their own homes. On a rational level, we know modern states depend on division of labor and the price mechanism for the economy to function. In the absence of a division of labor, no one will acquire the specialized skills we need to operate at the refined level of a modern state, such as vascular surgeons, piano tuners, or high-heel shoe designers. And given that people will be exchanging highly specialized goods and services with strangers, we will have to rely on the price mechanism to shape the growth of the economy in a rational manner—to avoid producing too many or too few items. However, the only way we can use the price mechanism to shape human behavior in a productive way is for people to own the things they produce or exchange with others.

The critic of my analysis might suggest we can eliminate price as an exchange mechanism, have everyone contribute their goods and services to a central committee for the greater good, and then distribute the goods and services to everyone based on some formula of fairness. The problem with this model is most people do not consume most of the products or services that are produced in a modern state economy and have no interest in them. For example, will people who do not like country or hip-hop music consider the people who produce these things as making a contribution to society? The reality is egalitarianism or centralized distribution works only if everyone partakes of nearly everything that is collected or produced, which is why bands or communes dedicated to foraging or subsistence farming can distribute things equally. Otherwise, if I make country music, how many units should I produce? If no one likes my music, do I still have a claim to the goods and services from central distribution?

To produce the "right" number of units, I need an objective feedback mechanism to tell me when to speed up or when to slow down production. I would propose that price is the only functional feedback mechanism (it processes the most relevant information) in a modern state where most people are strangers, assuming that the society is regulated by the free exchange of goods and services that are a function of supply and demand. Therefore, if I am going to take signals from the market when deciding how many units to produce, I have to own them if I am going to use them to exchange for other goods and services in the economy. In this way, private property becomes both a benefit and a responsibility—a responsibility to use our limited resources wisely and to not waste them on things people do not want or need. Once we remove private property from a modern state that is based on price and division of labor, we remove the rational mechanism that ensures we use our limited resource in a rational way. Otherwise, we will find ourselves in a situation where a product people want is not being produced enough and a product people do not want is being produced too much, which would leave us all worse off in a world of finite resources. The only way to rationally use our finite resources and minimize waste in a society of strangers is to rely on the price mechanism, which in turns presumes private property.

Only after we have found an optimal way to create wealth with limited resources does it make sense to talk about distributing wealth. That said, distributing a reasonable amount of wealth in a rational way can be a powerful way to ensure society stays on the narrow path for creating wealth, but only after we have created enough wealth to fuel the system in the first place. For example, infrastructure generally benefits society as a whole (roads, bridges, airports, etc.) and promotes economic growth and wealth creation. The same goes for other social spending: healthy, educated citizens from strong families are more likely to be productive members of society and less likely to be criminals or dependent on the state. However, although building a new freeway or building a new school might be good for the economy, there might be other projects that would be better for the economy and there might not be enough money to fund both projects. We always have to consider the opportunity cost of selecting one project over another, and not all projects have positive cash flow or result in a net benefit for society. The mere fact that some social spending can be called an investment (positive cash flow) does not mean all social spending is an investment. Likewise, the mere fact that some social spending can be wasteful does not mean all social spending is wasteful. We need the universal investment to distinguish between good and bad social spending.

INCENTIVES

The topic of incentives could fill volumes: how do we provide people incentives to do what they otherwise would not do? How do we provide people incentives to not do what they otherwise would do? How do we provide people incentives to pursue social or corporate goals at the expense of personal goals? The premise behind all of these questions is that humans do not automatically do what is in their best interest or in the best interest of society or institutions, for two reasons. First, in the context of refinement, people are not born biologically or rationally refined or mature and therefore need to be led carefully down the narrow path until they can walk on their own, which is usually done with carrots and sticks to achieve discipline and endurance. Second, in the context of society or institutions, their continuation demands from us things that detract from our own personal development and interests—the greater good, sacrifice, etc.—with the understanding that what we gain from our sacrifices often makes our lives better.

Therefore, when we consider incentives for people in society, we should remember we are often swimming against the current, and that the first goal is holding our position and staying afloat. We all benefit from individual refinement and social cooperation, but getting there is the hard part. These questions often involve psychology, economics, and other social sciences that collect empirical data to develop theories about incentives, but we should consider whether there are questions about the questions raised by the social sciences. For this chapter, we will consider incentives in terms of philosophy (universals and teleology) and private property.

If we begin from one perspective, people on the left often argue that the most refined individuals in society are generous and do not obsess about private property, and that we should admire these people and aspire to be like them in our own lives. If people in their most refined state are generous and no longer obsess about private property, then we as a society should aspire to eliminate private property because refined people have no need for it. The problem with this view is that it cuts to the chase of growth and maturity without going through the necessary and natural stages that are required to arrive at the desired end state (teleology), just as all good stories include new wisdom for the hero at the end of the story that would not be possible for the hero to understand without the painful journey.

From another perspective, people on the right often argue that ordinary people are motivated by greed or private property and that society will therefore benefit if we can channel this greed in a positive way, such as creating wealth and jobs. That is, if people are naturally greedy and motivated by private property, we should enshrine the idea of private property and make it a fundamental right that defines our economic system. The problem with this view is not all people are greedy and the amount of greed or self-interest they have is often a function of age and maturity. Just as professional sports teams identify potential recruits in a specific sweet spot of age, our wants and desires tend to follow a natural arc or pattern that individuals and society can exploit for the best consequences. As if often the case, both perspectives are right and wrong for different reasons because they approach the problem from the wrong perspective.

We should consider human nature in the context of private property and incentives, but we should also consider the kind of society we need (institutions, laws, economy, etc.) to create an environment in which people can fulfill their teleology. As I have claimed previously, people living at a band or social organism level of existence are living in an unrefined stage that makes it difficult to fulfill their teleology. This does not mean they are bad people or not deserving of rights; it is an observation and a prediction that these societies will probably never produce creative or innovative thinkers that shape human history. Just as a company or institution must grow beyond a certain size and level of complexity to achieve economies of scale that go beyond what individuals could produce on their own, society must grow beyond a certain population and level of complexity before people can fulfill their teleology, and this process is inextricably linked to the creation of wealth. We need sufficient material success to create the infrastructure to function with a high level of refinement, and the only way for this to happen is for the people who are in their prime working years, with a healthy desire for private property, to produce enough wealth to grow the economy. At the same time, these ambitious workers have to altruistically provide for children and the elderly. I addressed this topic in *The Political Spectrum* and will address it from another perspective later in the chapter.

The social predicament is this: to stay on the narrow path of social progress, we need working age people to be productive workers (even if they do not like their jobs) and to, within reason, place the needs of society above their own (paying taxes, delaying gratification, restraining their behavior, making sacrifices, etc.), but people naturally resist both. Left to our own devices, we have a tendency to take the path of least resistance and avoid social obligation for individual interest. This is not because people are naturally lazy or bad; it is because we are born into a state of limited refinement. Unlike other animals, humans often require two or more decades of hard work and discipline to reach the point of becoming productive members of society—the fine line of balancing the pursuit of their own interests and the interests of society. The "chicken or the egg" conundrum is exacerbated by the fact that we need refined individuals to lead us down the narrow path to reach biological growth and maturity—a complex and fragile situation.

One solution to the conundrum is trial and error. As people struggle to survive, they slowly learn what works and what does not work. There is undoubtedly some truth to this methodology, especially as it relates to surviving in a particular geography or climate. Another solution to the conundrum is the internal model of teleology. As we age, our body grows and develops, which shapes the way we think and behave, often regardless of our external circumstances. Improper nutrition stunts our development, but the body has an impressive ability to extract nutrients from food, evidenced by the countless number of cases of people who are raised in abject poverty and achieve impressive levels of success and refinement. Trial and error is obviously important, but I would suggest the natural growth and maturity of people (teleology) is an equally important factor in explaining how humans escape the social predicament.

Bringing this all together, we can now look at incentives in the context of private property. On the one hand, as I addressed previously, private property is required as a society grows in population and complexity. It would be impossible for over 300 million people in the United States of America to hand over all the fruits of their labor to a centralized place for equal distribution. Distribution in a modern state requires exchange; exchange among strangers in a modern state requires price; and price requires private property so that people can adjust production (increase or decrease) to ensure supply does not exceed demand or that demand does not exceed supply. Otherwise, people would blindly produce goods and services and hand them over to a central committee for equal distribution, even if no one wants them.

On the other hand, the key point of this section is the claim that our biological growth and development requires private property. If we recall our babies with toys and candy, humans in an unrefined stage of growth and maturity naturally grasp at objects and claim them as their own. If we promise a child a toy or a piece of candy, he will clean his room or do many things he would not do if left to his own devices. This simplistic example applies to adults as well. The human condition is such that we need people to struggle and work during their prime working years because society needs a mechanism of wealth creation to sustain itself. As luck would have it, people naturally strive and work hard during their prime working years, if they have been properly guided with carrots and sticks, because people naturally strive to possess and accumulate things, such as food, sex, trinkets, status, and power. If we want to keep people on the narrow path, there has to be a clear and fair path of success and there has to be a clear and fair set of rules to prevent other people from taking from them what they have earned—private property. In their golden years of retirement, people will probably reflect and wonder why they were so obsessed with accumulating private property, but the fire of competition helped them grow and develop in a way that made such reflection possible.

Not all people have equal abilities to acquire or create private property and some people have clear advantages, such as being raised by a wealthy family, so some inequality will be the inevitable result of a modern state. However, the alternative to this potential problem (no private property) is much worse. If we do not give people incentives that are appropriate to their stage of biological growth and maturity, as well as provide protections for those incentives (private property), then we should not be surprised if economic and social progress stumbles. One of the important points of this book is that the desire by some people to eliminate private property is nothing more than a primal desire to reject the burdens of the rational mind and the demands of a modern state. The proof of this is people are free in a modern state to form a commune and live an egalitarian life style with other like-minded people. The reason this does not happen more often, in my opinion, is the people who espouse these beliefs have benefited from a modern state and private property in such a way that the egalitarian life style in reality would be unbearable. Just as unrefined people at a band or social organism level could never draft a social contract to run a modern state, refined people in a modern state will struggle with returning to a more simple and less refined existence, especially during their prime working years when they are filled with ambition and dreams.

As we age and retire, the simple life might seem appealing again, but only because our fuel is running out and we are reaching the end of our productive lives. But if we are to have a satisfying retirement, we better hope the people in their prime working years are working hard to sustain society and continue making contributions to Social Security and Medicare/Medicaid. Humans and societies have a natural growth arc that is grounded in teleology, but whereas human life ends in decay and death, the growth arc of society should rise until it reaches optimal performance and remain there as long as possible as each new generation assumes control, a form of social immortality.

CASH FLOW

If we accept the need for private property in a modern state, then we should consider the idea of cash flow to gain new insights. Society, institutions, organizations, and even individuals live by the mathematics of positive cash flow. If a society does not collect taxes, the government will go bankrupt. If a company does not sell its products or services, it will go bankrupt. If an organization does not collect membership fees or donations, it will cease to exist. We cannot put the cart before the horse by presuming the positive cash flow and only later think about ways to collect it. In the business world, this would be like a technology company deciding it will sell one millions smart phones and then cajole or compel people to buy them, regardless of the demand.

These are the irrefutable laws of mathematics, which would not be possible without private property. A government, a company, a charity—none of these could exist if there was no such thing as private property, especially in a modern state with 350 million people. How could a technology company conduct research, produce products, and pay employees if there was no such thing as private property—if strangers could enter the business and take products without paying for them? What if we could go to Fort Knox and take the gold? Government is impossible without private property. Thus, private property is not an isolated abstraction to worship; it is an integral node of a complex web of universals that makes modern states possible. Removing private property from a modern state would be like removing spark plugs from a vehicle.

Before beginning, however, we should consider what we mean by cash flow. In a modern state, there is a tendency to think of cash flow as people exchanging dollar bills. There is some truth to this, but cash represents something tangible—the underlying private property that is being exchanged for other goods and services. The proof of this is that positive cash flow makes sense even in a world without cash. For example, consider a small town with a farmer's market where the vendors sell their goods to outsiders but barter among themselves. There is no fundamental difference between offering somebody $2 or three apples for a loaf of bread, as long as the person selling the bread accepts the trade. The proof of this is the person selling the bread could take the $2 and buy three apples from another person. Money merely facilitates a transaction when bartering is not convenient, but the money must be considered as valuable as the numbers written on it, such that we would be indifferent to having $2 or three apples if that is the price for three apples in a free market. Most societies use some form of money to facilitate the exchange of goods and services, but we should not allow this to cloud our minds about what is happening below the surface.

Cash flow comes in three forms: positive, neutral, or negative. In the case of positive cash flow, our income exceeds our expenses on an ongoing basis, such as a company that makes a profit. For example, if our all-in cost for producing 1,000 widgets (materials, labor, building, equipment, etc.) is $1 million, then if we sell those 1,000 widgets for $1.2 million, we will have positive cash flow (profit) of $200,000. Or, if we buy a bond that pays 4% interest, we will have positive cash flow, assuming we receive our initial payment when the bond reaches maturity. Needless to say, having positive cash flow more often than not is the best scenario for investments. In the case of neutral cash flow, we are usually talking about clubs, charities, or non-profit organizations. For example, if a chess club needs money to cover the administrative costs, the club can divide the total cost by the number of members and have each member pay a fair share. The club has no interest in making a profit but must balance the books to remain active. In the case of a non-profit organization, there is no attempt to generate profits, but this is a morally neutral term because one way to achieve this is to pay higher salaries. Non-profits have private property and often partake in the game of exchanging goods and services in a market economy, similar to for-profit organizations. The key difference is that there are no outside owners or investors who are hoping to make a profit from the venture.

As we shift to negative cash flow, the situation is more complex because negative cash flow can be indicative of a successful venture. Normally, if cash flow is negative, the image that comes to mind is a business that is losing money. If an entity is draining cash faster than it is taking it in, bankruptcy is the probable outcome. However, there are scenarios in which negative cash flow is part of a long-term plan for a successful business venture or investment. Consider a house. When we buy a house, we have negative cash flow—principal, interest, taxes, insurance, repairs, utilities, etc.—but if we select the right house, we might have a good return on investment. However, there is also a chance that the house will not sell for a profit, which is why negative cash flow investments are risky. Often, we run out of money before we can cash out for a profit. As the saying goes, the market can stay irrational longer than we can stay solvent.

The most important point for this section is the best way to think about our own biological growth and maturity is as a negative cash flow investment, which is why being successful in life is all about the long game. From the time we are born, we consume resources (food, clothes, toys, etc.) without offsetting positive cash flow. In fact, many people remain in a negative cash flow mode well into their adult years to pay for their education. One of the biggest challenges is that we never know which negative cash flow investments will pay off in the long run. In fact, we know many of them will not pay off. For example, many aspiring athletes invest time and money to make it to the big leagues and most never make it. We can agree or disagree on whether pursuing a dream like this is worth it, but the fact remains many pursuits are negative cash flow and we all have to work to pay the bills before we catch a break.

The most important point for political philosophy is who is responsible for funding or assuming the risk for these negative cash flow ventures? One of the grievances about wealthy families is their children are thought of as having unfair advantages. This might be the case (having wealth is an advantage), but more often than not, the family ends up funding the negative cash flow ventures, not society. They are using their own money if the venture does not succeed, which is often the case for some professions. In the case of everyone else, we know life is usually negative cash flow for the first couple of decades, but to what extent does society have an obligation to fund or offer loans for these negative cash flow ventures for individuals who cannot afford them, especially if the odds of success are low? If society has the obligation to pay for people to go to college, does society also have the obligation to pay for people to roll the dice for a career in professional sports or writing? The important point is as long as we are in a negative cash flow mode, we are net consumers of private property. And if this negative cash flow is funded with debt, we are consuming future private property—moving demand forward, all of which I will address in more detail in the next chapter.

Escape Velocity

When we observe how people behave, over time and in different societies, we can detect patterns that give us insights about people and society. The reason for this is no matter how much societies grow or develop, the bell curve distribution of refinement tells us the majority of people in any given society will be focused on working hard to pay the bills and put food on the table, with limited leisure time or wealth accumulation. Although individuals grow and mature, societies tend to be more sticky and focused on people paying the rent and eating.

Societies do progress, but not with the same natural arc we see for individuals. In fact, we can talk about a society or institution with a natural growth arc before reaching a plateau to sustain itself.

If we observe less developed countries, we tend to see individuals or groups fighting for control over the limited positive cash flow institutions or assets, to include the government, which is frequently one of the best means of enrichment via corruption. If we observe more developed countries, we tend to see more individuals and groups striving to create wealth and start new economic ventures, with government work viewed as less prestigious, but we also see individuals and groups fighting for control of positive cash flow institutions and assets and preventing rivals from overtaking them. For example, an individual might try to get a high paying job with a Fortune 500 company or a company might put in a bid for a contract for drilling rights to oil on federal land. That is, even though developed countries have often succeeded by promoting the American dream of starting a new business and creating wealth, our economy is still dominated by powerful positive cash flow institutions and assets.

Some ambitious people pursue the entrepreneurial dream, but the majority of people will opt for a path of less resistance and economic security. This is not negative or surprising because humans are risk-averse, meaning we demand a higher return on ventures for assuming more risk. If life in a state of nature is nasty, brutish, and short, then many people seek out the security that goes with working for established positive cash flow institutions or assets. Likewise, given the wealth and power many of these positive cash flow institutions and assets have, people also seek to jump ranks to get to the top or take them over, such as a new government winning an election and granting plum positions or big contracts to friends. As much as we promote the American dream of starting a new business as a path to wealth and success, there are natural limits to the number of new business ventures a society can absorb at any given time, just as there are natural limits to the number of divas who top the music charts, and there will always be larger businesses taking steps to keep new competitors out of the market—barriers to entry. In theory, the world could find space for another laundry detergent or energy drink, but many markets are saturated. Not to mention, success often depends on luck, timing, and a confluence of events in society and technology. Just look at what the digital revolution is doing to the music and publishing industries in terms of digital music and books. The point is we have millions of people clamoring for the most coveted, high-paying positions in our society, and many people would just as soon take advantage of whatever advantages they might have than play fairly by the rules.

A common complaint today is that being born rich is an unfair advantage. Historically, the sons of wealthy families attended Ivy League schools, received gentlemen Cs, and assumed plum positions in the family business or on Wall Street with other "club" members. They were often catapulted to the top of the social pyramid without working their way up the hard way via meritocracy, if such a path could even be said to exist for people outside the "club." There is no doubt some of these individuals would not have been selected for their jobs in a world of free competition, but the criticism of "unfair" ignores the fact that people in a free society may spend their money as they choose, assuming they do not break any laws to earn the money.

Children in wealthy families have advantages, but mostly because their parents invest heavily in their negative cash flow ventures—diet, education, clubs, travel, and so on—and offer them good jobs. In many cases, they outperform most people in society, and society needs high performing people to assume the most difficult jobs, just as professional sports teams recruit the best players to win championships. They can afford the golf lessons at the country club and the creative writing classes in Florence, all of which have tangible benefits. Besides, many of these wealthy children do not succeed in their ventures, and then it is the family that loses money, not the government or society. The simple fact is that if a person owns a successful business and hires his sons, daughters, or friends, even when there are more qualified candidates, that is his choice, his liberty. There is often more to life than hiring the most qualified candidates or giving opportunities to strangers, such as keeping wealth in the family and being surrounded by people whom you know and trust. Besides, if business owners make a habit of hiring the wrong people, the businesses probably will not survive and other businesses will rise up to replace them.

In the case of minority populations that do not feel part of the system, one solution is for the wealthier people in those minority populations to establish businesses that provide jobs for people in their minority group because this is what all the other groups of people do around the world. To look at the issue from another perspective, if a poor family were to win the lottery and use some of the money to send their child to a good university, would this be fair? If a middle-class politician who complains about the privilege of wealth subsequently acquires wealth while in office and uses his position to get his children into good universities, would this be fair? People should be free to dispose of their private property as they see fit, and institutions should be free to hire and fire as they see fit, with the understanding we will all face scrutiny in the court of public opinion.

I could continue this analysis, but we should now transition to an idea I call escape velocity, which I will define as an individual or institution that manages to escape the grind of accumulating one unit of wealth at a time to having enough wealth and capacity to actively shape the market or society. In the case of an individual, this usually manifests itself in the person achieving mastery in his work, whether plumbing, athletics, medicine, or writing. In the world of mastery, there is no easy path to perfection. Mastery takes time and effort (maybe 10 years, or 10,000 hours, and so on, for those with the right natural talents), often in a negative cash flow way. For example, many writers or artists toil and sweat for years or decades for the eventual big pay day, even after they achieve mastery in their skill. Mastery is not required for financial success, and many people with mastery will not have financial success, but achieving mastery should be an important part of the process of growth and maturity. No one is born to do a particular job, in the same way ants and bees are born to do a particular job, but some people are more predisposed to certain types of work based on their personality, character, natural talents, and so on. Society benefits via division of labor when individuals achieve mastery, and individuals benefit from achieving mastery because it gives us insights into life and gives us a better opportunity to live a comfortable life because of the quality of our work.

In work, the benefit of achieving mastery or escape velocity is that the quality of the work improves dramatically but with less loss of energy as the person makes the transition from rigorous conceptual thought (discursive) to spontaneous, intuitive thought (non-discursive). As a result, the person usually derives more satisfaction from work. On a personal level, achieving escape velocity allows a person to tap into the more creative depths of life rather than scrounging for the next meal, which should be viewed as positive, but there is also the danger of losing one's edge. People who live in artificial escape velocity, in the sense of having the wealth but not the mastery to sustain it, such as spoiled children, lack the resistance or pressure that comes with real escape velocity; this hinders them from achieving mastery. Granted, living in escape velocity is often one of the best ways to achieve mastery, such as writers with patrons to sustain them, because it allows them to focus, because it allows them to focus on the task at hand, but there is something to be said for making it to the top the hard way and making sure we never allow wealth to satisfy our hunger.

As we shift to escape velocity in the context of institutions or assets, the situation is different because institutions and assets are not organisms, like cells or humans. Thus, when we speak of society, institutions, or assets achieving organic growth, we are speaking metaphorically. If we recall that a modern state is not an institution (not a social organism), because it serves no specific purpose, we will focus on institutions and assets, which are designed to improve performance and achieve specific goals. Consider a varsity football team. The goal of this institution is to win, along with other benefits, such as being part of a team and maturing in the fire of competition. In support of this, the coach will recruit the best players and train them to win, with the understanding that a team with players who work hard and hustle will often defeat teams with more natural talent, using the 1980 U.S. Olympic hockey team as an example. Most people will not make the varsity team, no matter how hard they try, but the student, teachers, and community can enjoy and celebrate a victory. People who are not good enough have no claim to be on the varsity team, and the coach should reserve the right to make personnel changes to make the team better. If we consider a coach who fails to make these difficult decisions for the greater good and the team loses the championship as a result, the families from that school should reserve the right to find a new coach.

To be clear, not everything in life is about winning at all cost, but if we want stay on the narrow path of social progress, we should expect and demand that our most important institutions and assets focus on winning because the world is filled with competitive institutions and assets ready to take their place. Individuals have the right to demand some slack from society, but that right does not extend to institutions or assets. It would be improper for people to demand a job over a more qualified person, regardless of any hardships they might have overcome. Granted, wise institutions care for their people and look beyond GPA, test scores, and last names, but only to the extent that it improves the overall performance of the institution. If we demand that institutions hire less capable people or do not allow them to fire less capable people, we will make these institutions less capable, just as a varsity football team would not perform as well.

CONCLUSION

If I am successful in this chapter, the reader will take away the key points that social progress is possible and that social progress is necessarily linked to the introduction of private property. Conversely, to the extent that society moves toward eliminating private property, social entropy will be inevitable because the absence of private property was our original state—the band or social organism. If there is such a thing as Utopia or social perfection in a large and complex modern state, private property will be an integral part of it. This does not mean private property should be worshipped blindly or that granting private property status to something is always the best thing, but if we consider human teleology and the nature of the material world we live in, the only way to provide humans the incentives they need to improve their lives is to give them ownership over some aspects of their lives that allow them to work their own magic. We all benefit when individuals and institutions succeed, but individuals and institutions will be less likely to take the risks associated with achieving success without the right incentives because humans are naturally risk averse, as science confirms. As we develop the idea of private property, we see it is not a detached idea to revere; rather, we see it as an important universal that is a key node in a complex web of universals that make rational life possible in a modern state.

CHAPTER FIVE. EQUALITY

The idea of equality has been prominent in political philosophy during the modern age. Some of the city states of Ancient Greece practiced democracy, in terms of one man, one vote, but citizenship was limited and the economies often rested on slave labor. As is often the case, then and now, some people were more equal than others, and it is not an exaggeration to say most societies throughout history have not embraced the idea of equality, at least not as we understand it today. Even in the Unites States of America, with the first lasting Constitution dedicated to the idea of equality, suffrage was not universal until the twentieth century. Some people were more equal than others: you were equal if you were a white man over 21 years old who owned land. This was apparently considered progressive during this time.

Despite all this talk about equality, as Fukuyama has argued, a nation should be careful about implementing universal suffrage too soon, for the same reason that large corporations like Apple and Exxon do not rely on popular vote by the employees for selecting leaders or making strategic decisions. Mass opinion does not always result in rational decision-making, so popular vote is not always the best way to select leaders or make the best policies, but democracy is based on the idea that the leaders of a country should reflect the will of the people, and the best way to achieve this is with some semblance of equality within the population. As I will address in chapter seven, the idea of equality fits into both the liberty (freedom from oppression) and fairness (proportionality and the law of karma) moral receptor buckets, but this chapter will focus the ideas of equality of outcome and equality of opportunity.

The first step is to address what we mean by equality. If you ask ten random people to define equality, you will probably get ten similar but different answers because it is an abstract universal that has developed over time from one society to another. Like the word love, equality means different things to different people; and even if we gain a more precise definition of equality, we will learn there are different kinds of equality—equality of opportunity, outcome, intelligence, capabilities, etc. For the purpose of this chapter, we will consider what most people mean or believe they mean when they use the word equality in the context of political philosophy.

If we consider people in terms of height, weight, intelligence, abilities, shoe size, income, and so on, it should be clear that people are not equal as a matter of fact. After all, each person has unique DNA and therefore cannot be equal; even identical twins grow up to be different in many ways. We should not let this bother us because serious people do not think about equality this way in political philosophy. If we consider that people themselves are not equal, in the same way that apples and apples are equal or oranges and oranges are equal, then we should consider the circumstances in which they can be thought of as being equal.

The first example is the claim that people are equal "in the eyes of God." If God created the world and loves each of us, then he should love all of us equally. As the Apostle Paul said, "For God does not show favoritism." Not all people will accept or reciprocate God's love, and it is not logically inconsistent to talk about God passing harsh judgment on us even if he loves us, but the idea of God and religion make sense only if we are all equal in the eyes of God.

The second example is the claim people are equal "under the law." Historically, people have not always been equal under the law, to include many countries today. For example, in the Leviathan of Hobbes, the sovereign enforced the law but was not himself subject to the law, which is known as rule *by* law, as opposed to rule *of* law, in which case all people, to include the sovereign, are bound by the laws. The idea of equality under the law is relatively new and many modern states, including the United States of America, are struggling with holding rich and powerful people accountable for their actions, even those in violation of the law. This type of equality is a work in progress and aspirational, and if it ever reaches a rational expression, the punishment people face for crimes will reflect their position or power. As we entrust our fellow citizens with positions of power and trust, they should be held to a higher standard with harsher punishments for their crimes, rather than the common practice of a slap on the wrist.

Most people in modern states probably accept the idea of equality "in the eyes of God" and "under the law," so this is not where we should expect to find any major disagreements in political philosophy. Not to mention, both of these forms of equality are mostly negative in the sense that we do not receive anything tangible. Being equal in these two senses prevents negative things from happening to us—being treated unfairly by God or being treated unfairly under the law. If we are equal in the eyes of God, then we will be loved equally and treated fairly. We will not receive special benefits like miracles or a free pass to heaven if we refuse to repent—give unto God. If we are equal under the law, we will be treated equally and fairly. We will not receive special benefits like titles of nobility or vast tracts of land, and we will face fair and just punishment for our crimes—give unto to Caesar. Therefore, when we consider the more contentious idea of equality in the context of political philosophy, we should consider the idea of equality in terms of receiving tangible benefits, such as money or resources.

ALIENABLE RIGHTS

If extraterrestrials were to watch television or read newspapers for many countries today, they would probably conclude that many humans believe they have a right to almost everything. It is a rare event indeed when someone does not invoke the word "right" when discussing a controversial issue. A short list of rights includes the following: life, liberty, the pursuit of happiness, property, vote, marriage, income, education, college, abortion, birth control, job, livable wage, healthcare, respect, Internet access, dignity, cell phones, and the list goes on. The problem with expanding the list in such a way is it is difficult to understand where we draw the line, which makes it difficult to define what rights are. What do these things have in common? What principle do we use to identify our rights? Obviously, we cannot all have a right to everything, without reverting to a band or social organism level of existence without private property. If you claim a right to something tangible, then other people should also have the same right to it and can take it from you after you receive it. If you have a right to an apple, then you can take one from the local fruit vendor, even if you do not have money, but this in turn means anyone can walk into your house and take the same apple from you; having a right to an apple amounts to nothing if we implement this principle consistently. Therefore, we should analyze the list of rights to identify essential points and gain clarity on this issue.

One of the most important points about private property is that we have to understand it in the context of finite resources. If resources are infinite and available to all, there is no need for private property. Therefore, when we think about rights, we have to consider whether private property is involved. The reason for this is obvious: if resources are finite and all people have to a right to something, how do we make sure everyone gets it; and for those who do not get it, on what basis would we deny them the right to take things from others? The other part to consider is this: if we have a right to something currently not available, then someone else will have to provide it to us, meaning some of our rights become obligations for others. For example, if we claim a right to life, then this means no one can take away our life without proper justification, such as self-defense or punishment for a crime. The right to life does not grant us anything tangible in terms of private property or benefits. However, if someone claims a right to food, then others will have to provide the food. The "others" could be the government, but the government would have to take it from the taxpayers.

To explain the difference, imagine going to a remote island with a small community. If the right could transfer with you, it is one kind of right; if it could not transfer with you, it is another kind of right. If you have a right to life, you can still have the same right to life on a remote island. However, if you claim a right to Internet access or college, this will not work on a remote island, and it is therefore a different kind of right. The distinguishing feature is whether private property is involved. For our purposes, therefore, we will define a right as anything we have a claim to, in all times and all places, that does not involve receiving private property from the government or other people. Thus, rights are essentially negative; or, at a minimum, our language should include a universal that is defined as having a claim to something that does not involve private property, in contrast to the idea of having a right to something that is private property. If we claim a right to something, it is something others cannot take away from us, such as our life, our liberty, and our pursuit of happiness.

If we claim there are circumstances in which we have a claim to private property or tax revenue, such as education or healthcare, then we should use a more appropriate term—entitlement. Not only does this term make better sense; it reflects current usage and differs enough from the idea of rights to merit a distinct term, which goes a long way toward clearing up the confusion in the debate about rights and entitlements. When governments discuss budgets and spending, they talk about entitlement spending, not rights spending. The idea is that if you are entitled to something, you will receive a tangible benefit, like money or a service. For example, if we pay into Social Security and meet the minimum requirements, we will be entitled to receive monthly payments after we reach retirement age. Granted, most or all of the money we receive is money we paid into the system (and many people leave money on the table), so the program should be thought of as mandatory retirement savings, not taxes or entitlements, but we will continue to receive payments even if we withdraw more than we paid in over the years. If the government does not collect enough money in taxes to fund these programs, the government will borrow money by issuing bonds, which is another way of saying deficit spending. Our $20 trillion deficit should serve as evidence that our political process lacks the discipline to keep spending under control. Modern states should have entitlements, but because they necessarily involve the collection and transfer of private property from the citizens who pay taxes, we have to manage them rationally and according to the laws of mathematics—return on investment, opportunity cost, etc.

When we consider entitlements in the context of equality, we can talk about reasonable minimum standards that do not force us into deficit spending. For example, if we want to live by the principle that all children deserve a good education, which most modern states accept because educated citizens generally become productive, tax-paying citizens who are prepared to satisfy their social obligations, then we should be able to honestly assess our society and economy to develop an educational program that meets some reasonable minimum standards. This way, the students who finish the school program will have the skills to help sustain society or move society to the next level of complexity and refinement, with the understanding that many people will not satisfy the minimum standards and many people will exceed them.

If the education standards are too low, social progress will be sluggish because the students will have a difficult time taking complex jobs after graduation. On the other hand, if we aim too high with our educational standards, relative to our current stage of social or economic development, we could hinder social progress by draining too much wealth from the system (opportunity cost) and preparing the students for jobs that do not exist. In this sense, by guaranteeing every child a school that meets minimum standards, we could be said to have equality. This is not the same thing as saying everyone will have the same quality of education or that everyone will have the same educational results, because students are not equal and wealthy people will send their children to private schools or pay for tutors. If we consider human nature and the world we live in, however, this might be the best we can do. The big challenge is defining the minimum standard.

In theory, we have enough smart people to reach consensus about which subjects to teach at school and at what age, as part of the organic growth and maturity of the students, but unfortunately the education of our children often falls victim to politics. I will not propose any specific solutions to improve our public schools, which have steadily eroded as spending has steadily risen (relative to other developed countries), especially in poor neighborhoods, but I will highlight that equality in education can mean only one thing in political philosophy: establishing a minimum standard that each child is entitled to and can be tested against to measure progress. Giving every child an identical education in a modern state, especially with hundreds of millions of people with vastly different backgrounds and levels of income, is impossible and unreasonable. By minimum standards, I mean what is required to keep children on the narrow path of biological growth and maturity, with the understanding that people will have to avoid things like substance abuse or other suboptimal behavior if they hope to succeed.

The corollary to this is the financial return on education in terms of jobs and economic growth should be positive, like an investment, rather than a net drain on the economy. What this means is that any attempt to offer developed-country educational standards to a country where the average person has a fourth-grade education will probably fail. It takes time, sometimes generations, to make the transition to modern state status, depending on the political will of the people.

One way to measure educational standards is to assess whether there are enough good jobs waiting for college graduates. If college graduates cannot find good jobs, year after year, we are probably sending too many people to college or too many people are studying the wrong subjects (supply and demand). The best solution is to focus on training people for the right jobs, which might or might not require a college degree, or focus our resources on growing the economy to create the kinds of jobs college graduates can fill. Good jobs will not magically appear just because we train people to do them; but if we grow the economy to create good jobs, then we can send more students to college to fill them—we're back to the chicken or the egg. Just as we have to create wealth before we distribute it, we have to create jobs before we train people to do them. This same logic should apply to all entitlements: as a modern state, we have enough smart people to devise minimum standards for many aspects of life that we can fund with current tax revenue in a way that promotes economic growth and prosperity.

GIVE OPPORTUNITY A CHANCE

The previous section naturally raises the idea of opportunity in the context of equality—equality of opportunity. As life makes abundantly clear, people are not equal as a matter of fact, which means the pursuit of equality of outcome (same education, same skills, same talents, same income) is not a reasonable or viable option. Even Rawls, one of the champions of modern social justice theory, recognized that equality of outcomes was not possible, even in a just society. We can take steps to ensure the less fortunate and less capable receive the tools and resources they need to do the best they can, but the outcomes will still vary, often dramatically, from top to bottom within the social pyramid. That said, just as we can talk about achieving equality by providing minimum educational standards for all children, we should consider what we mean by equality of opportunity.

People in modern states have largely reached consensus that all people should be allowed to pursue all opportunities, at least in theory. If people are so inclined, they should be allowed to pursue admission to a school, a position on a sports team, or certification for a career, and so on. No one should be prevented from selecting a seat on the bus. Some opportunities might be limited by age, gender, nationality, professional certifications, and so on, and many people will fail in their pursuits, but on the whole, opportunities should not be limited artificially or by decree. For example, the U.S. Air Force sets age, height, weight, and vision standards when selecting pilots, rightly so, but as long as these age, height, weight, and vision standards are met, the U.S. Air Force should not randomly deny officers the opportunity to at least apply for a position. Many people will not be selected, but this is fair if the process is fair.

However, if extraterrestrials were to observe us, they would probably conclude many people on earth believe they are being denied the right to pursue many opportunities. As mentioned previously, we should specify where we are seeking an opportunity before assessing whether we should have the opportunity to pursue it. In the case of society, we are all equal under the law and we should all therefore have the opportunity to pursue whatever is offered by society—attending public schools, registering to vote, applying for a passport, owning a gun, applying for a driver's license, and so on—unless we violate laws that limit our opportunities. A society has a right to set standards for these opportunities, such as passing a driver's test or registering to vote, but the standards should be reasonable and applicable to all. In the case of an institution, however, especially one based primarily on performance and profits, such as a sports team, an Air Force fighter squadron, a university, or a private company, everyone should have a theoretical opportunity to pursue membership, but the needs and standards of the institution should outweigh the needs of the individual. There is a good chance a person will not be accepted, but this does not mean the person has been unfairly denied an opportunity. If a sports team has any interest in winning, it will recruit only the best players and the best coaches. Therefore, even if we are good by objective standards, we might not make the team because everyone else might be outstanding by objective standards. In this case, our right to pursue opportunities will not have been denied.

In the case of organizations and other groups in civil society, people should have the opportunity to start a group or request to join a group, with the understanding the organizations should reserve the right to set parameters on membership, such as age, gender, profession, and so on, even race and ethnicity, as long as these organizations are not associated with the government (although the government is full of groups and organizations defined by race and gender). If a group of Irish men want to start a dart club, they should be free to do so, even if it means excluding everyone else.

All of this might sound great in theory, but many people would object that some historical grievances have to be addressed before we can unleash the full power of freedom and liberty. After all, our founding document, the Constitution, provided structural benefits to white men and structural disadvantages to black people that had a lasting legacy. For example, if elite public universities and elite publicly traded companies select only white men only because they are white men, not because of their qualifications, then these white men will gain an unfair advantage that will shape society. This, in turn, will promote a vicious cycle over generations with the possibility of less capable white men making their way to the top of the social pyramid and more capable minorities being artificially pushed to the bottom of the social pyramid. This legacy remains in some places, but the steps society can take to address these historical grievances will be limited by freedom and liberty and the choices people make. The business owner's son might not be the right person for the job, but the job is the business owner's to offer.

The only way the state could address this problem to the satisfaction of many people would be the creation of authoritarian government controls to compel and coerce people to behave in certain ways throughout society, both inside and outside the legal system, which no modern state would accept as a solution. We can enforce equal opportunity where the government has such control, such as giving people access to public schools, but we cannot force people to give opportunities to people with their own resources. If two white men want to start a law firm, they should be free to do so, even if they benefited from a legacy of white male privilege and deliberately have no plans to hire minorities. Likewise, if a group of rich white women decide to hold a weekly book club, where they discuss business opportunities that benefit them at the expense of others, we as a society would be out of place to force them to invite minorities. We could rightly question their desire for racial insularity, but ultimately we have to respect their choices.

The proposed solutions to this problem tend to divide the population into two political camps. Whereas progressives on the left argue the state should intervene in society to level the playing field or reduce inequality in the name of "caring," even at the expense of the other five moral receptors I will raise in chapter seven, social conservatives on the right focus on balancing all six moral receptors, even in the face of inequality, because of a belief that a failure to account for all six moral receptors will result in a loss of social capital, which will exacerbate inequality. We should accept that people overall and the left and right have noble intentions, so our analysis should focus on how the policies of the left and the right play out in the real world when passing judgment.

If we agree there are limits to what the government can do to compel people to change their behavior, there are many things the government can do to change the way people think. If we agree that people being subjected to systematic poverty is a big part of the problem, then in addition to giving people more opportunities, we should also take steps to change the culture that contributes to preventing people from achieving their full potential. As history has shown, only cultures that embrace hard work, discipline, delayed gratification, strong families, and wealth creation have a chance of walking the narrow path of social progress, which is something each generation must learn anew.

Although many groups have struggled with fully participating in the American Dream, due to a variety of circumstances, providing these individuals opportunities is only the first step. The other reality is that many of these individuals find themselves living in a culture of poverty, such that the culture itself makes it difficult for them to escape the poverty to take advantage of opportunities. If people grow up surrounded by drugs, crime, and a culture that does not celebrate academic success or delayed gratification, then they will have a difficult time taking advantage of many of the opportunities society has to offer them. The government can promote a culture of success and provide a system of incentives, but people have to make the choice.

As long as liberty and fairness prevent the state from imposing drastic social change, which should be the case in a modern state, then the individuals and groups that are struggling will have to assimilate the culture of success if they want their shot at the American Dream.

STEERING THE SHIP

In response to the perceived legacy of white male privilege since the writing of the Constitution, some people have invoked words like diversity and inclusion to steer the ship of society in a new direction by attempting to change behavior and ways of thinking. Within a modern state, people should not receive unfair privileges based on race or gender; and just as we may have to steer the ship in a new direction to reverse historical grievances, such as investing in low-income neighborhoods, it should be with the goal of treating all people fairly, not with giving unfair privileges to new groups.

As it stands, attempts to steer the ship is often in a reactive mode: if white men have received unfair privileges in history, then the proposed counterbalance solution is often to offer unfair privileges to women and minorities, such as implementing quotas. The obvious problem here is two wrongs do not make a right and does nothing to solve the underlying problem. The more reasonable and challenging solution would be to eliminate any unfair privileges white men might be receiving, whether legally or informally, and move on to the business of holding people to the same standard. If we all demonstrate a willingness to take the high road and allow merit to determine the decisions we make as individuals, as institutions, and as a society, there will be no need for groups to seek unfair privileges, either in the private sector or the government.

With diversity, the general idea is institutions and organizations benefit from reflecting the broader population. Institutions and organizations benefit from a diversity of skills and personality types to achieve the division of labor that is necessary for success—the whole is greater than the sum of the parts. In this sense, the benefits of diversity are obvious, and it makes intuitive sense that women and minorities will be motivated to reach for the stars if they see women and minorities in positions of power and influence. Unfortunately, the motivating idea for diversity has focused too much attention on race, gender, or other identity politics categories. For reasons that are not clear, the argument is that merely adding women or minorities will automatically create the same benefits of true diversity, regardless of skills or personality types. Statistically speaking, we probably are likely to increase the true diversity of a group by adding more women and minorities, but the increase of diversity is not automatic because it is possible to have racial and gender diversity but limited diversity for skills and personality types. Likewise, it is possible to have true diversity with a group of white men if they have the right mix of skills and personalities. For institutions or organizations that have an historical legacy of limited diversity and want to reflect the broader population, some proactive steps probably will have to be taken to break the cycle.

In the case of inclusion, even if we achieve diversity in terms of having a good mixture of skills, personalities, genders, and races that reflect the broader society, some people might feel reluctant to take the initiative and some bosses might not give their people the opportunities to show what they can do. For example, in an office with an alpha male boss, shy or introverted workers might be reluctant to speak up, and the boss might be less likely to give them good projects or a chance to speak up with their ideas, which is not good for the organization. Science has proven the value of introverts, but the challenge is making sure organizations give introverts the chance to demonstrate their skills and talents. The idea of inclusion is that in addition to promoting diversity, institutions and organizations should take active steps to tap into the full potential of each person, which in theory should improve the overall performance of the organization.

In the abstract, this sounds like a positive idea that any leader should embrace, but it suffers from one setback: the emphasis on expecting institutions or organizations to cater to our individual needs, rather than changing our behavior for the greater good of the team. To use a sports analogy, any coach worth his salt will know the individual players on a personal level and will tailor the coaching to the needs of the individual players, but at the end of the day the players need to perform and put the needs of the team above their own needs. Sometimes we have to work against our natural grain to help the team succeed, just as we do in life. If someone is naturally quiet and shy about speaking up, this should be recognized as a growth area for the individual, not as an obligation for the team to accommodate.

Given that many people think white male privilege still dominates our society today (keeping in mind all the poor white men who are dying from opioid addiction), it is not surprising that terms like diversity and inclusion are prominent in political philosophy. The problem with this focus on white male privilege is that it tends to overlook an important fact: the world is ruled by the adage, "it's not what you know, it's who you know." Many hiring and membership selection decisions are based on networking or referrals, and these formal and informal networks tend to be more homogeneous and less diverse than most people are willing to admit. Why hire a complete stranger if there is a known quantity? If a particular company has a recent history of hiring white men, there is a good chance these white men were within the Kevin Bacon six degrees of separation.

Likewise, many people who attend Ivy League schools can seek out and receive good job offers, but some of these students are from well-connected families with good jobs already waiting for them. It is not clear how well they would do by shopping around their resumes. Although Ivy League schools are like clubs, not all people who attend are members of the club or will have good jobs waiting for them after graduation. If we want the rules of the game to be fair, women and minorities should expect white men to select them for positions about as often as women or minorities select white men over women or minorities for positions they oversee. In an ideal world, we would all make a concerted effort to move beyond our comfort zone and expand our horizons, but we should all start this journey by looking in the mirror. My guess is that a company run by women to promote women in business would not like being told they have to hire white men in the name of diversity.

In the Genes

A common narrative of the equality of outcome view is the idea that all people are potentially equal, but for nurturing. They admit human nature is real, kind of, but claim it is the same or nearly the same in all of us, and could never account for the vast differences in human abilities or income we see in the world today. The argument is not often articulated this way, but this view suggests that if we were to remove a group of randomly selected newborn babies from around the world, ship them off to an enlightened society on a remote island, and give them the best upbringing possible in terms of diet, education, love, and encouragement, then all the children would rise to roughly the same level of performance and success. Some might be poets and some might be doctors or scientists, but none of them would end up as drug addicts, criminals, or social outcasts, or so the theory goes. Throughout history, whenever politics shifts to the left, there is talk about removing children from their parents to usher in Utopia.

Many us of rely on this thought process when we look at someone who has not been successful or has resorted to crime or other problematic behavior—if only they had been raised in a better environment. There is some truth to this narrative, of course, but there are countless examples of people raised in abject poverty who succeed and people who were raised in opulent splendor who fail. Like the social contract theory, this mental exercise seems to make false and idealistic assumptions that the evidence does not support. Something other than nurture also accounts for how we grow and mature—nature. As I have argued in this book, teleology shapes the arc of our growth and maturity and allows us to say what it means to actualize our potential with a degree of objectivity, but there is also a nature piece of the puzzle that has to be accounted for. Our DNA also plays a key role in shaping the kind of people we become and how well we perform.

The first problem with the nurture narrative is—so what? Even if we agree that children, all things being equal, will have a better chance of success if they are raised in an ideal remote island environment, the relevant point is we do not have enough resources to provide every child this ideal remote island experience. Even if we did, this would mean a disproportionate number of adults would be dedicated to grooming these children for success and not performing all the other jobs and social functions that make a modern state possible. In other words, such a plan would not be sustainable. As we reflect on our own lives, we can always ask, what if? Perhaps we could have been an Olympic athlete or a drummer in a jazz band, if only we had attended elite training programs as a child, but at whose expense? If we could go back and redirect resources to those projects that would have helped us, who would have lost out?

Most people never rise to the pinnacle of the social pyramid, even people who participate in elite training or education programs, so we might find ourselves worse off or wasting resources by giving too many opportunities to too many children, especially if most of them end without success. The majority of people will find themselves living in the bell curve distribution of refinement, which means most people will have to make due with what they have and hope their hard work and grit will eventually give them a break. The bell curve distribution is stubborn and resists change, and pumping more money into the system will not result in significant changes unless the culture changes as well. The culture of poverty perpetuates poverty, and there are many cases of people winning the lottery and ending up poor a few years later.

People have to achieve a certain level of personal refinement if they hope to live at a certain level of social and professional refinement, keeping in mind that personal refinement does not mean wearing a business suit. The other harsh truth is there will always be many naturally talented children (nature) with enough family wealth to attend the elite training programs, which will facilitate their rise to the limited number of coveted positions at the top. If we are truly caring and concerned about children with less than ideal environments or talents, we would start them on the path of learning the practical job skills that all societies need and for which unusual talent or elite training programs are not required. Most people with a good work ethic and discipline should have successful careers if they dedicate themselves to the long game of mastering a craft.

The second problem with the nurture narrative is it leads us down the path of breaking the natural bonds between parents and children, which I addressed in *The Political Economy*. One of the clearest findings of the social sciences is that children who are raised by their biological parents have a distinct advantage over children from broken homes. For this reason, all people, regardless of political affiliation, should actively promote the traditional family with the same level of intensity that they actively promote education. The reason for this is the strong bond of love and altruism that exists between parents and children and does not exist anywhere else in society and is an essential ingredient to growing into mature adults. Strangers will not consistently make the sacrifices children need to grow and mature. Some people might feel excluded by this family model or find it too traditional or oppressive, but the benefits to the children should outweigh any personal beliefs some people might have on the topic.

In a free society, parents have a right and an obligation to raise their children and their children have a right to be raised by their parents, which means many children, even ones fortunate enough to be living with both parents, will find themselves living in the bell curve distribution of refinement. Some children might benefit from being separated from their biological parents in terms of preparing themselves for their future, but it would strip away the rights of the parents and children to experience one of the most meaningful and satisfying experiences in life—raising children in a family. Do we work to live or do we live to work? Granted, we could address this problem by providing all children with great schools in their neighborhoods, but family life and culture are equally important, if not more important, so we will still have a situation in which children from broken homes will be at a disadvantage to children from traditional homes.

The third problem with the nurture narrative is it downplays the importance of, well, nature. Studies with identical twins prove that nature and nurture both play important roles, with some studies suggesting an overall 50%-50% split and others suggesting upwards of a 70%-30% for intelligence in favor of nature, so we are doing a disservice to ourselves and society by focusing our efforts on nurture at the exclusion of nature. The specific numbers are beyond the scope of this book, but the point is when we look at children in less than fortunate situations, in addition to asking how changing their environment could be beneficial for helping them achieve their potential, we should also ask what, if any, genetic factors might limit their potential. If a professional athlete has children and trains them from a young age to reach professional status later in life, then although we can rave about the benefits of the environment the child was raised in (wealth, training, etc.), we can also rave about the genetic variables that contributed to the child rising to professional status.

Obviously, we should not relegate children to the "no potential bin" just because they are born into poverty or with drug-addicted parents (after all, the parents might have been the victims of a bad environment), but we should always consider nature and temper our expectations when our nurture investments do not work out. Spending more money often does not help. For example, just as we should consider nurture when trying to break the cycle of domestic violence (the assumption being that the behavior is learned), we should also consider nature (a genetic propensity for violence). All things being equal, the benefit of the doubt should always go to the nurture and potential side of the debate, for sure, because even if we are predisposed to some undesirable behavior, such as substance abuse or violence, the ability of people to achieve self-mastery and transcend these limitations speaks well of the human spirit.

I had the good fortune of growing up in a nice suburb in Minnesota where everyone was middle-class and "above average," to quote Garrison Keillor. Yet, there were dramatic differences in performance, from academics to sports to what people did after high school. Nature and teleology play an important role in our biological growth and development. A rose will benefit from the right amount of water, sunlight, and soil, but even if a rose lacks the optimal amount of water, sunlight, and soil, it will bloom into a rose. Humans are resilient (or antifragile, as I will address in chapter seven), and our nature and teleology, not our environment, determine what we become. Whether we eat beef or chicken, wheat or corn, whether we read Homer or Virgil, Defoe or Nabokov, our bodies will extract the relevant nutrients and blossom naturally. As psychology has demonstrated, much of our hardwiring takes shape before we start kindergarten. Therefore, although we should improve high schools in poor neighborhoods, the battle was in many ways lost before it began. I would propose that if the goals are fairness and helping children achieve their potential, then we should have an honest discussion about the importance of the traditional family and take tangible steps to promote it as the ideal social model.

Franchise Economy

Some readers might conclude that my analysis is one-sided. This book promotes a moderate social conservative view, it is true, so in this sense the book is one-sided, but this is with the purpose of making an argument for my view, not to attack other views. My views are the result of the conclusions that follow from my analysis of universals and teleology; I did not declare my views and then manipulate my analysis to bridge the gap. Just as we cannot help but conclude that all A are in C if we know that all A are in B and all B are in C, my arguments follow from a set of foundational beliefs resting on intuitions that cannot be proved but can be shown to be cohesive and consistent. I am mindful, though, that wealthy or privileged people could view my philosophy as a green light to justify their wealth or privilege, which is not my goal by any stretch of the imagination. Just as I believe many people looking up the social pyramid suffer from resentment, I believe many people looking down the social pyramid suffer from a lack of compassion and leverage their wealth or privilege to fast-track their children to the top of the social pyramid. The social conservative view focuses on ensuring society is positioned to create wealth, not to insulate wealthy people from competition. As a result, it is appropriate to address an issue I believe contributes to social inequality and stifles the free exchange of goods and services in the context of building an entrepreneurial culture.

One of the mathematical realities of life is that society benefits from scaling and economies of scale as well as sound business models that have the potential to succeed (because many business models are doomed to failure from the beginning). If we want to make the transition from a band or social organism to a modern state, we have to find a way to grow our production in a non-linear way such that we can double production without doubling our work. Such a transition is not possible without division of labor, the price mechanism, and private property, as well as other important universals like value, cash flow, assets, liabilities, debt, equity, and so on. We require increased division of labor to refine the skills that are required to run a complex company, and we need private property to have control over production. If there is no private property and people are free to enter our factory to take our inventory, we will have no incentives to offer our labor to help the company. Modern states still have to address what kind of monetary system to have, who will control interest rates and the money supply, who will grant government contracts, and so on. As long as there are opportunities to profit at the expense of others, as long as there are opportunities to abuse political power for financial gain, as long as people expect to get paid more than the true value of their labor, we will have to curb the excesses of human behavior.

A good way to begin is with an example many people can relate to—beer. Anyone who has tasted beer knows craft brews are usually better than most brand name mass production beers. In many cases, a person with the right equipment can brew perfectly good beer to sell on the local market. To produce a national or international beer, however, a massive business infrastructure is required, to the point that many of the employees are not directly involved in making beer. There is nothing wrong with creating new jobs to support such an effort, but few of these functions are required for society to produce enough quality beer to satisfy demand. To make matters worse, to brew a beer with national or global distribution, it is usually necessary to add preservatives so the beer does not spoil during the lengthy distribution channels, whereas a local brewer can sell beer without preservatives direct to the consumer.

There is no doubt that building brands is one of the goals of business and we should not pass laws to outlaw them, but the economies of scale for beer brewing do not add to the quality of the beer beyond a certain point. In fact, the economies of scale often reduce the quality of the beer beyond a certain point. Brewing beer is like making porridge: not too hot, not too cold—just right. The brewing operation has to be big enough to produce a quality beer but not so big that preservatives have to be added and the quality begins to drop, especially when lower quality ingredients are used to save money. For anyone who appreciates beer, the appeal of a label should never take precedence over the appeal of the product, except for people whose sense of identity is derived from the products they consume or want other people to see them consuming. In the case of industries that require economies of scale to improve the quality or to make the business model viable, such as electronics or automobiles, this makes sense. Society benefits from the establishment of these large corporations, but there are many cases in which the pursuit of economies of scales seems to be an end in itself, which makes it more difficult for small entrepreneurs to enter the market and compete.

The same thought process about beer also applies to other businesses, in particular, business models that operate as franchises. If we consider the businesses that do not benefit much from economies of scale—sandwiches, hamburgers, coffee, haircuts, dry cleaning, and the like—we see that a large part of our strip mall economy is dominated by franchises, many of which make their profits due to a tested business model, often with lower quality products and low wages. I am not proposing we should ban these franchises, but society at different levels (city, country, state) should reserve the right to establish zoning laws to decide which types of businesses will and will not be allowed, as long as the decisions are based on a principle of fairness and quality of life for the community and not on corruption, for three reasons.

First, some franchises allow outsiders who will have limited or no involvement in the business to be the owner, with some people owning dozens of franchises and managing them from a distance. In many cases, these franchises have high entry costs that limit who can make an investment, whereas a small business loan should be sufficient to open a shop to sell sandwiches or coffee. Most communities would benefit from local owners running their own businesses because it keeps profits in the community for a family unit rather than sending them to a corporate headquarters in another state or country and paying the locals at the minimum wage.

Second, many of these products, such as fast food, are unhealthy (in excess) and therefore are a net negative for the health of society. Granted, you get what you pay for and many people benefit from the dollar menu, but these restaurants have lowered our dietary standards. Third, the low wages paid by these jobs means many workers will earn minimum wage, which is fine for students and retired people, but many adults have these jobs as well. There have been calls and protests to raise the wages to $15 per hour, but most of these business models would fail and file for bankruptcy. In the case of a family-owned business, however, family members who are living with the owner (the profit center) perform many of the job functions that pay minimum wage, but they partake of the profits via the family. Many of these minimum wage jobs are not designed for bread winners, and a hardworking person should be able to rise to the ranks of management, but many of these franchises create barriers to market entry.

If many of these franchises did not exist, many of the jobs would not exist, which would hurt many people who are satisfied working for minimum wage with part-time hours, such as students or retirees. The best way for people to avoid the minimum wage trap is to acquire job skills that pay higher wages, but franchises holds significant sway in an economy that create barriers to market entry for the small guy. Wealthy people with limited knowledge of the business can invest money in relatively low-risk ventures, which in turn closes the market to many competitors. Consumers in a modern state based on liberty are free to choose where to spend their money, but most people prefer the quality and feel of mom & pop shops, and selectively excluding certain business models, like franchises, will result in more mom & pop shops opening. It is not a coincidence that many nice communities do not have fast food restaurants or megastore mall complexes. Fast food restaurants and brand name coffee shops are not common in Italy, but the country is filled with spectacular restaurants and wonderful cafés that sell shots of espresso for one Euro, not to mention the family vineyards that sell wine and olive oil.

To summarize, many franchises, due to their market share and franchise fees, create barriers to market entry for small entrepreneurs or business models that often do not benefit from economies of scale. A small restaurant owner can make a pastry just as well if not much better than a large corporation. Some franchises require the investor to play an active role in running the day-to-day business, which is a positive development. We need large corporations to make electronics, automobiles, or dig wells for oil, but we do not need them for many other businesses that line the streets where we live. At the end of the day, however, only consumers can demand these changes. If people support local businesses and place a premium on craft and quality, then the franchise model in many cases will be less viable.

CONCLUSION

Many people are born with advantages (wealth, talent, etc.) and many people benefit from luck, but just as Hume asked the law of causality for its credentials, we could ask equality for its credentials. Where does this idea of equality come from? We identified some areas were most people agree about equality, such as "in the eyes of God" and "under the law," but this does not address many of the historical grievances. We also identified other areas of agreement regarding equality, such as the idea that opportunities should not be artificially denied or that groups benefit from having a variety of skills and personalities, but there are no seeds in these ideas that would justify a move toward authoritarian controls to enforce equality. Society can intervene to prevent people from abusing their wealth or disrupting the free exchange of goods and services, but we should not throw away the baby with the bath water by disrupting the system of incentives that makes wealth creation and modern states possible.

Chapter Six. Liberty

Along with the idea of equality, the idea of liberty has a prominent place in modern political philosophy. Any discussion of political philosophy would be incomplete without a detailed analysis of liberty, to include how it shapes society and how we live as individuals. Most people along the political spectrum, on the left and the right, who would otherwise disagree on most issues, speak positively about liberty, at least in the abstract, which means there must be disagreement about what liberty means. Just as people on the left and the right do not agree on issues like abortion or guns, due to their conflicting core beliefs, the only way both sides of the political spectrum could support the idea of liberty is to have different understandings of what it means. As I will address in chapter seven, the most important difference is the progressive left thinks about liberty in terms of the government protecting us from the excesses of the private sector, whereas the libertarian right thinks about liberty in terms of protecting us from the excesses of the government. Like the other important universals in this book—teleology, culture, private property, equality, and so on—liberty is a universal in a hierarchical web of universals that holds together our views of the world in a cohesive and consistent way that allows us to make rational decisions in our lives with important consequences.

Just as we cannot move along the narrow path of social progress without division of labor, private property, and a price mechanism to facilitate the exchange of goods and services among strangers, we cannot progress to the level of a modern state without liberty. People will not achieve specialized expertise in all the various job skills required for a modern state without liberty. A nation without liberty would results in many important jobs not being filled with qualified people and would lack the dynamism and creative destruction that is required for progress. In many cases, human liberty is limited in the early stages of social development—in a band or social organism, there is no liberty to speak of—but the narrow path of social progress requires increasing levels of liberty until we reach the point where we can create a social space where liberty has a place of honor after we have satisfied of our social obligations. Paradoxically, although liberty is an essential ingredient for social progress, liberty also sets natural limits on social progress because part of liberty involves taking time to enjoy life and make choices about which challenges we will or will not pursue. This is why the pursuit of Utopia requires increasing levels of authoritarian power.

Humanity's march toward liberty seems inevitable because it reveals the natural unfolding of our teleology from potential to actual. The narrow path of social progress seems to lead toward eliminating oppression and slavery, the opposite of liberty. Neither Hegel's dialectical idealism nor Marx's dialectical materialism can satisfactorily explain liberty or the narrow path of social progress, which is the natural yet not inevitable result of humans fulfilling their potential. As the human organism grows and matures, the quest for liberty unfolds because it reflects our natural state, if by natural we mean in accordance with our teleology. The liberty receptor is hard-wired into our brains. This is an empirical claim we can see with our own eyes throughout history, such as the American and French Revolutions and the Arab Spring. Even if all of this is true, however, we still need to explain what liberty means, which will most likely lead to serious disagreement among the believers of liberty on the left and the right.

I will begin the analysis by saying what liberty is not: liberation or emancipation. Liberation and emancipation are important ideas in political philosophy; everyone who is oppressed or enslaved wants to be liberated or emancipated, and they are accompanied by a feeling of liberation when it happens. Many of the greatest moments in history involve people being liberated or emancipated in various ways, but these two ideas represent reactions to a negative situation, not something we strive for in itself, similar to how curing a disease is not the same as good health. We seek liberation or emancipation from oppression or slavery, but they are not natural ends we strive for because once we achieve liberation or emancipation, the need to pursue them goes away. However, some people view liberation or emancipation as a perpetual process—long live the revolution! They are the perpetual opposition that has no idea how to govern. Also, we can achieve liberation or emancipation and still not have liberty.

Liberty is something real, something tangible, especially at the pinnacle of civilization.

The primary mistake of thinking about liberty in terms of liberation or emancipation is the old Rousseau mistake of believing man's natural state is the noble savage living in a band or social organism—that society or institutions hold us in chains. Society and institutions can hold us in chains, especially in an authoritarian government, and in this case we are justified in seeking liberation or emancipation. However, we should remember that society and institutions are the only means by which humans achieve the kind of biological growth and maturity that makes liberty possible. The noble savage is not in his natural state, if by natural we mean in his most refined stage of biological and intellectual development. In a state of peace and prosperity, liberation and emancipation do not exist because there is no need for them; however, liberty not only exists in a state of peace and prosperity, it is essential to it, defines it, and must always be nurtured and defended, lest we risk losing it.

SOCIETY: THE UN-INSTITUTION

To continue our analysis of liberty, we should review possible places where we might find it. As I have addressed before, we can broadly consider three areas: 1. society as a whole, 2. profit- or success-focused institutions, and 3. civil society or personal fulfillment organizations. (Obviously, we will not find liberty in the state, which exists to protect the realm of liberty.) To understand what society is, we should begin with institutions (2), which we have defined as collections of individuals pursuing specific objectives such that the whole is greater than the sum of the parts. For example, consider a business that sells a product to make a profit, a law enforcement agency that conducts investigations to bring criminals to justice, an army that trains to defeat an enemy, or an orchestra that practices to play the classics for an audience.

The first point is the collective activity of institutions achieves something that could not be achieved by individuals acting alone, due to division of labor. For society to progress from a band or social organism to a modern state, we have to find ways to pool our resources and talents to achieve what we cannot achieve on our own. The only way for society to progress is for individuals to achieve a level of expertise in certain skills or talents because we cannot be experts in everything. We need some people to dedicate their time to medicine rather than hunting. We need some people to dedicate their time to fixing cars rather than gathering berries.

The second point is that this can be achieved in an institution only if the needs of individuals are subordinated (sacrificed) to the needs of the institution. We have to set aside some self-interest for the good of the team, or the institution will be nothing more than a collection of individuals. If individuals in institutions demand too many benefits or accommodations, or if the institution chooses new members who are unable to perform at the right level of expertise, the organization will decay and performance will suffer. An orchestra is only as good as the collective quality of the individuals that are selected. One person terribly out of tune will ruin the performance for everyone. Giving a less competent person the opportunity to join the orchestra might be good for the person but would not be good for the orchestra or the audience.

Granted, these institutions will not succeed if they force members to sacrifice everything for the greater good (I say usually because the slaves who built the Egyptian pyramids were successful in their endeavor), and many institutions do better if they give people space to grow and develop as individuals. However, from a system perspective, the mission of the institution must come first and then people must be selected to fulfill that mission. A group of talented individuals can agree to work together first and find something to do second, but they will have to subordinate some of their personal interests to improve the capability of the team. To repeat, institutions that put "people first" will often perform well, even better, but only to the extent that putting "people first" is a pragmatic means to an end of achieving institutional success.

The important point is true liberty is not generally found in these institutions, which is why liberty is not possible in a social organism: the entire society performs as an institution, much like an ant farm or beehive. People with liberty will be free to seek out which institutions they try to join, and the institution might help them develop in ways that makes liberty more satisfying, but they will take the liberty with them to the organization. They will not discover liberty within an institution, at least while they are actively participating in the institution, unless their personal goals and ambitions perfectly align with the institution. If a person finishes work at a factory (institution) and goes home at the end of the day, he will potentially enter the space of liberty. This does not mean submitting ourselves to institutions is always bad or that life should always be about seeking a perpetual state of liberty bliss, because liberty is not the absence of personal responsibility, but all people would benefit from understanding what liberty is, where we find it, and where we do not.

Where this becomes important is when people believe an institution is the space of liberty and make demands on the institution such that their personal development and satisfaction are more important than the mission of the institution. When I was in the Air Force, this was never a problem because my fellow airmen and I never dared to think for even one moment that our needs took priority over the mission. We used words like mission and sacrifice, which was our way of saying we put the mission above our own needs. We could throw our hat in the ring for certain jobs or opportunities and derive satisfaction from the work we did, but the mission came first. If people cannot find a way to find satisfaction in the mission of the institution, they should probably seek another institution, rather than self-absorbedly ask the institution to accommodate them. Granted, the mission of an institution often inspires people to do their job well, and satisfied people usually but not always perform better, but my fellow airmen and I never had any illusions about why we woke up each day. Institutions have problems when people take priority over the mission, when individuals try to carve a space for liberty within the institution. Imagine a professional sports team or world-class orchestra that started hiring sub-performing individuals or allowed the members to tell the coach or conductor how much they are willing to practice. As long as the mission is clearly defined and people are expected to conform their behavior to the needs of the institution, the institution should be well positioned to face competition from other institutions.

Shifting to society, this is where we find the space of liberty, but we have to focus our lens because the space of society and the space of liberty are not the same thing. If we imagine a population of people living within a defined geographic territory and ruled by a government that has a monopoly on coercion (the definition of a modern state), then the space of liberty is found outside the state and outside the institutions that are required to sustain society and make social progress possible. However, just because we are outside the state or institutions does not mean we are in the space of liberty because society also has demands on us that we have to satisfy in the same way that institutions make demands on us. Two of these social obligations, the prohibition of deficit spending and the sanctity of monogamous procreation, are the most important topics of *The Political Spectrum*, and need not be repeated here.

With this analysis, we can now define liberty as the social space we enjoy on our own terms after we have satisfied our institutional and social obligations. The social space of liberty often includes civil society but it is not the same thing as civil society because liberty includes many individual or solitary activities. After a long day of working and taking care of the children, or during the weekend, liberty is the space where we are free to do what we want, which might include joining clubs or organizations or taking classes for our career.

As simple as this might sound, this is where the debate begins because it raises the important question: What are we allowed to do with this liberty? One of the most common ways of defining this space is the idea that consenting adults should be allowed to do whatever they want as long as they do not violate the law or the rights of others. This is a decent definition for liberty that many people might accept in the abstract, until we propose specific situations that might raise concerns. For example, under this definition, things like incest (among cousins), polygamy, drug use, and prostitution would be allowed, and yet most public discussion on these topics leans toward prohibition or criminalization. These issues can be debated and the consenting adults argument is not without faults, for sure, but we should shift our attention to the most important space for this discussion: the right to associate and criticize.

If we believe in liberty, in the sense that all people should have a space where they can claim liberty, then people should be allowed to associate with whomever they choose and criticize whomever they choose within the space of liberty, even if wise people collectively agree that this behavior is not admirable. If a group of Hindus want to form an organization for recreation or to discuss maya and karma, liberty should allow them to form such an organization, at the exclusion of others, and this same right should apply to everyone else. The argument could be made that life is more rewarding if we integrate ourselves with many people to experience the full diversity of our country, but this does not change the fact that liberty means we cannot be required to do so.

Likewise, the same idea applies to criticism. If a group of Hispanics decides to protest Columbus Day, in response the atrocities Columbus committed against the native populations in the New World, they should have that right, as long as they demonstrate in accordance with the law, without violence, and respect the right of others to celebrate Columbus Day as a federal holiday. The same idea applies to members of the KKK, fascist parties, or communist parties. All reasonable people would prefer that these groups not exist, but liberty dictates we must allow them space to express themselves, primarily because this is the best way for others to show them the errors of their ways. We can ignore them, criticize them, ostracize them from our own groups, but we cannot prohibit their right to free expression.

The conclusion from this is a society defined by liberty will inevitably have behavior and spoken words that some people find offensive or in bad taste, but any attempt to stop this would be a violation of liberty and would take us down a path that would be less desirable. Any attempt from the far left to aggressively promote its political agenda would eventually be offset by an attempt by the far right to aggressively promote its political agenda. People on the left are often offended by people on the right, but people on the right are often offended by people on the left, and the two sides will probably never see eye to eye, which is precisely why liberty and rule of law must rule the day. We must allow election results and the rule of law determine how we live. This does not mean truth is relative or there are no correct answers to the questions of political philosophy, but it does mean we cannot impose our beliefs on others in the realm of liberty. The solution to this predicament is both sides of the political spectrum recognizing that being offended is a fact of life and that any person or group that defines itself by being offended as a way to exert itself within society should be ignored.

Although the way some people act or express themselves under the banner of liberty might be unfortunate, and we as a society should shun those who lack civility, especially if it involves coercion or intimidation, but an even more unfortunate development would be a movement to restrict liberty with the ostensible goal of eliminating this unfortunate behavior. We see movement in this direction with things like "political correctness," but the more accurate term would be "violating people's liberty to protect liberty." In a society where liberty has a proper place, we must tolerate intolerance, as long as this intolerance is peaceful and does not interfere with the rights of others, keeping in mind that intolerance is often in the eyes of the beholder. An individual feeling of outrage does not rise to the level of national concern.

Words and behavior are not offensive just because we say they are. If a dozen Irish guys at the paper mill form a darts club, they have every right to deny membership to someone from Vietnam, just as African Americans reserve the right to tease white people about how they dance. This trend toward instituting political correctness or things like "hate speech" is an unfortunate move in the direction of a social organism, the opposite of social progress. In the space of liberty, people are allowed to choose their friends and offend other people. The good news is we have 330 million people in our country, so everyone should be able to carve out their own spaces of meaningful liberty where they can feel comfortable and associate with people with shared views and interests. As the saying goes, we have to respect the rights of other people to disagree with us if we are going to expect others to respect us.

Opinion Entitlement

If we accept that liberty allows us to do things not everyone will admire, such as limiting who we associate with or passing judgment on others, we also have to accept that people will hold false beliefs, or beliefs that are impossible to prove one way or another. Many discussions result in a dreaded conclusion: "everyone is entitled to an opinion." Although many arguments are grounded on beliefs that cannot be proven, rational people explain why their beliefs merit consideration. The other challenge is that when people argue about important issues in political philosophy, they often invoke different sets of core beliefs that conflict with the core beliefs of others, which makes mutual understanding difficult or impossible. There are two effective ways to defeat someone in an argument when these disagreements arise: first, show why their argument is logically inconsistent; or second, show why their core beliefs are not valid. This is a long-winded way of saying we could resolve most philosophical discourse by defining our terms and explaining our core beliefs, but the most important issues of political philosophy are emotionally charged and emotions often dominate the debate.

A recent technique to discredit opponents in political debate is to accuse them of denying science. If something can be proven by science, people should accept the finding, obviously, but this is where the fun begins, for three reasons. First, science is not capable of addressing many of the issues raised by political philosophy. The important issues in this book—universals, teleology, culture, private property, equality, and liberty—are in many ways philosophical and beyond the realm of science. Science can facilitate our philosophical knowledge, for sure, but science cannot answer the big questions of political philosophy. The claim that all true statements can be verified by science is not a scientific claim; it is a philosophical claim that happens to be false. We reflect on the abstract ideas of political philosophy with the power of the intellect, but exactly how this happens is beyond the scope of this book.

Second, science has had significant paradigm shifts throughout history, even during the twentieth century, and there is no reason to assume the current standard model of physics will rule the day in 10 or 100 years. Science has made limited progress in solving the "origin of life" or "origin of consciousness" problems, for example. Third, people often cherry pick data that supports their arguments, especially in the social sciences, rather than allow the collective findings of science to shape our ideas. For example, the fact that so many self-proclaimed intellectuals refuse to acknowledge how important the traditional family is for raising children, which is a scientific fact, is proof that filters on the left and the right prevent us from seeing the truth. Therefore, even though science has had successes throughout history and we would all be wise to integrate the findings of science into political philosophy, we should understand that the findings of science often do not apply to political philosophy and that people often invoke science in unscientific ways.

Shifting to a controversial issue, consider global warming or the hedging term climate change. On this topic, like many others, the two sides of the debate are often talking about two different things. The people who are generally outspoken about affirming the dangers of climate change focus on the negative consequences for the world we live in, such as ecological damage, which should concern everyone. On the other hand, people who are generally outspoken about denying the dangers of climate change focus on the negative consequences of implementing the proposed policies to combat climate change, such as reducing the consumption of carbon fuels. In fact, this group often argues the climate change agenda is nothing more than a shrouded attempt to implement a radical political agenda that is opposed to capitalism.[3] If we consider that the vast majority of energy humans consume in the world comes from carbon fuels and that global agriculture depends significantly on carbon fuels and petroleum products to grow our food, then any plan to dramatically reduce our carbon footprint would result in a global depression and mass starvation, which should concern everyone as well.

There are two reasons to be skeptical of the policy proposals for addressing climate change with dramatic cuts in carbon fuel consumption. First, some of the most important conclusions are based on computer models that have largely failed to make accurate predictions. If the theory or computer models were correct, the models would be more accurate and the world would be warmer now. We should look to the evidence, not to the computer models, to assess the theory. Second, unlike other areas of science, many believers of climate change refuse to consider debate in a way that is inconsistent with the spirit of science, which understands that science is never settled. No true scientist worth his salt would ever make the ridiculous claim that a scientific debate is settled, unless they are willing to claim the debate about the traditional family is settled. Even worse, some of the adherents of climate change have threatened to pursue criminal

[3] http://www.unric.org/en/latest-un-buzz/29623-figueres-first-time-the-world-economy-is-transformed-intentionally

charges against people who speak out against their claims, which is reminiscent of the Spanish Inquisition or Salem Witch trials. Some of the people speaking out against climate change agenda probably do have nefarious intentions, such as corporations that profit from pollution, but the pursuit of criminal charges is beyond the pale.

Shifting the other way, whereas the left often accuses the right of denying science, the right often accuses the left of denying mathematics, which is a more serious charge because mathematics is settled. For example, people on the left often say more money should be spent on social programs, such as education or welfare, which is a great idea in the abstract because no one (NB: no one) wants children to miss school or poor people to go hungry. However, these programs have to be funded with tax revenue, which has to be collected from the wealth of the citizens, so we have to consider how the collection of tax revenue will affect the economy and whether there is enough money to fund the programs. When people on the right raise concerns about spending for social programs, they are not questioning whether children should go to school or whether poor people should have food; they are questioning whether it is possible or sustainable.

Just as it bothers people on the left when people on the right say, "I believe in creationism, and everyone is entitled to an opinion," it bothers people on the right when people on the left say, "I believe we should raise spending for welfare programs, even if the money does not exist, and everyone is entitled to an opinion." People on both sides of the political spectrum are not always consistent—the predictable errors they make are indicative of their political biases—but even though we can say people should have consistent beliefs and should "follow the argument wherever it leads," the blessings of liberty guarantee that people will often believe whatever they want, which makes political discourse all the more difficult.

Rednecks & Welfare Queens (Nash Equilibrium Part I)

I previously raised the bell curve distribution of refinement, the idea that the (statistical) majority of people in any society work hard to make ends meet and do not have the time, resources, talent, or luck to rise to the top of the social pyramid or participate in the more refined activities of life like the arts, letters, and sciences. As a result, we tend to see the rise of subcultures or stereotypes that tend to be categorized as falling under one political party or the other, with both sides accusing the other of having a less refined voter base. For the left, they define the right as uneducated rednecks with Confederate flags and NASCAR. For the right, they define the left as uneducated welfare queens who avoid responsibility. Again, rather than discuss important issues in a serious manner, both sides resort to belittling the other side to discredit their core beliefs. After all, if the right is a bunch of redneck racists with Confederate flags, they cannot be trusted to hold higher office or offer opinions on policy issues. Or, if the left is a bunch of lazy welfare queens who live off the work of others, they cannot be trusted to hold higher office or offer opinions on policy issues.

Marx's most valuable insight was that our material circumstances, economy, and technology play an important role in shaping how we develop and grow individually and socially. These inputs can steer us toward a suboptimal way of living that is difficult to escape, especially after we start down the wrong path, like a vortex, and often in ways we are not aware. For example, agricultural societies tend to take a certain shape and promote certain values and coastal trading society tends to take a different shape and promote different values. The structure and values of these societies will often change in predictable ways with material, economic, and technological changes. Likewise, a society where the dominant technology is coal-fired factories will tend to take a certain structure and promote certain values but an information society will tend to take a different structure and promote different values.

Some of this has already been addressed, but the goal of this section is to revisit this idea through the lens of Nash equilibrium, which is a theory of games that relates to how non-cooperative people make decisions. For example, if we consider a prisoner's dilemma in which two suspects questioned by the police have a rational incentive to not finger their partner in crime, the police can offer incentives to motivate one suspect to finger the other to build a case. Given that criminals often cannot trust each other, despite honor among thieves, they might both finger the other suspect in the hope of getting away free, only to find themselves in a worse situation because both are convicted of the crime from the testimony of the other. Thus, the police can structure the interrogation to play one suspect off the other to get the best results, factoring in human nature and how people make decisions when faced with various positive and negative outcomes.

The important part is rational decisions are not made in a vacuum; we have to make rational calculations about what we think others will do and plan accordingly, to include factoring what we think they think we will do, and so on. For example, even if a president does not want to launch a war on another country, he might make the rational decision to do so if he has reason to believe the other country might attack first. If he attacks first, he saves his own country, but he might kill innocent people if the other country had no plan to attack. On the other hand, if he does not attack and the other country does, then his country might get destroyed and he will be judged for failing to take action.

Nash equilibrium also applies to society. As people find themselves living in suboptimal circumstances, they will often make suboptimal decisions about how to live, decisions that weave their way into the social fabric and shape the way future generations live. For example, if a society lacks modern farming equipment and needs manual labor to work the fields to feed the population, the odds are good we will see the rise of small group of wealthy landowners and a large group of poor workers to tend the fields, often with peasant or slave status. Once this pattern of behavior begins, it is more difficult to change over time because people become accustomed to living this way, both rich and poor, and the people on the top find ways to secure their grip on power.

For example, sugar cane farmers in the Dominican Republic established a system of importing workers from Haiti, often illegally, and subjecting them to slave-like working conditions in bateys. For many decades, this was the only way to satisfy global sugar demand. However, with the rise of modern farming equipment, such as tractors, many Dominican sugar farmers decided to continue with slave-like labor from Haiti because the transition to technology, which would have freed the Haitian workers from their terrible situation (to return to Haiti with no jobs), was seen as too difficult or too expensive. Not to mention, the children of these Haitian workers lacked the education to succeed in life and found themselves needing work as they grew into adulthood. Thus, this social and economic system developed into a suboptimal equilibrium—Nash equilibrium. Each year, the Dominican farmers knew how many new workers to import, and the government agreed to treat them as illegals to prevent them from demanding higher wages or social benefits. Each year, many poor Haitians knew this was their only chance to make some money to survive. Observing this from a safe distance was the witting U.S. government that was interested in ensuring global sugar demand was met.

Shifting to a less unfortunate example, we should consider a scenario in which free people make suboptimal albeit rational decisions in response to material, economic, and technological circumstances. If we accept that the world will probably never eliminate exploitation or coercion, because societies will always contain people in the middle of the bell curve distribution of refinement, we can talk about people living in suboptimal conditions even if they are free by modern standards. For example, if we consider what many people unfortunately refer to as redneck culture, we see people who enjoy things like NASCAR, trailer parks, sunburns, American flags, mullets, macaroni and cheese, country music, or two-stepping. These are perfectly fine things and activities that many fine people enjoy, but together they embody redneck culture.

Even if we assume that these people have no interest in science, art, literature, philosophy, foreign cinema, or other things that self-proclaimed refined people enjoy, we should ask—so what? If we accept that many people will find themselves living in suboptimal conditions, it should not surprise anyone that people seek satisfaction and fulfillment in suboptimal activities. The important question is, is the culture self-sustaining? If we were to isolate them and have them fend for themselves, would they continue to survive in the same way? Do they have a mechanism to produce the resources they consume? Do they have a mechanism to create and raise the next generation? If so, if people are satisfying these basic needs, then they should be given the space of liberty to live this way with the full respect of other citizens. As a society, we might look for ways to redistribute some wealth to improve their schools or provide incentives for businesses to create more jobs where they live, but as long as they have found a way to establish a symbiotic relationship with the world, are paying taxes, and obeying the laws, we should respect the customs and traditions they live by and understand that the framework is complex and fragile.

The same logic, however, does not apply to the welfare queen stereotype. Suboptimal patterns of behavior are also the result of people trying to survive in a particular environment if they are artificially sustained by government assistance. There is no doubt that modern states should have welfare, to provide temporary assistance to people who are often victims of the creative destruction of capitalism. However, this should be with the understanding that providing perpetual welfare payments and removing people from the fire of competition will have negative consequences, for the individual and for society. I am reminded of the story of the man who cuts a butterfly out of a cocoon to help it, only to find out the butterfly cannot fly because the struggle of escaping from the cocoon was precisely what the butterfly needed to develop its muscles property. Just as many people recognize that spoiled children of rich parents often never gain the necessary discipline for success and continue to live off their parents, people who are raised in systematic welfare often never gain the necessary discipline for success and continue to live off the state. And because these policy decisions have practical considerations, they should be judged by the results, not by intentions.

A welfare queen culture will develop around a system of perpetual welfare (not short term welfare) that will make it difficult to break the cycle. The welfare payments that were once a helping hand to get people back on the narrow path have become entitlements. However, given that this culture is living off society and is not a net contributor to society, this is not the space of liberty because the space of liberty assumes people have satisfied their social obligations. Thus, when we compare the stereotypes of redneck and welfare queen culture, it should be clear the two are not equal.

Many rednecks abuse welfare and many welfare queens break the cycle of dependence, which is why my analysis focused on stereotypes and does not apply to every individual. In the middle of the bell curve distribution of refinement there will be a variety of groups that achieve varying degrees of success in term of satisfying their social obligations. With all its faults, redneck culture prides itself on self-reliance, whereas welfare queen culture does not. The first step to resolve a problem is to recognize the problem. We should ignore cries from the right to eliminate all welfare but we should also ignore cries from the left who see nothing wrong with welfare culture and play on people's good sentiments. There is a big difference between spending money to help children get a better education and spending money to keep a healthy adult out of the labor force because the welfare benefits exceed the wages of a job.

ORGANIC DEFRAG

Whereas the previous section focused on how the human organism adjusts itself to material, economic, and technological circumstances, often in a suboptimal, Nash equilibrium way, this section will focus on how the human organism develops, often in a suboptimal, Nash equilibrium way, using a computer metaphor. Back in the early days of personal computers during the early 1990s, I was fascinated by the Norton defragmentation program. I could watch it for extended periods of time and take satisfaction as the hard drive was magically cleaned up and organized, like removing unwanted papers and books from a bookshelf and lining up the remaining books in a neat and orderly way. The visual display was a two dimensional array of small squares in rows and columns with different colors depending on the status of the square—empty (light blue), filled with movable data (dark blue), or filled with unmovable data (yellow), the latter of which resided on the ground floor and was usually reserved for large programs that could not be fragmented, such as the operating system. Normally, the individual squares would be filled with data from the bottom up, like constructing a building, with the unmovable data on the bottom providing a foundation.

The first step of the process was to analyze the hard drive, which would spawn the visual display of colored squares. Frequently, the hard drive was a mess. As programs and files are loaded onto and deleted from the hard drive over time, they often become fragmented to fill open spaces, with some bookshelves full, some bookshelves with gaps, and empty shelves near the top to give you a picture of how much storage space is available. Sometimes, the hard drive was so crowded there was not sufficient space to accommodate some large files in one space, so the large files would be fragmented to fit into the available small spaces, with instructions at the end of each slice regarding where to find the beginning of the next slice. This would be like taking a thick book and slicing it into five smaller books to fill five small spaces in the bookshelf, if there is no single place on the shelves to accommodate the entire book. Computers can work quickly, but a cluttered hard drive would slow down as the computer searched for the different slices of the book or created new slices as the file grew in size.

The second step was the defragmentation process. The program would collect the various slices of the fragmented files, move them to a large open space near the top, recombine them into a seamless file, and move the other files around, like sliding books to one side to make room for the large book. At the end of the process, the hard drive would look organized, with the yellow squares on the bottom, the dark blue squares in the middle, and the light blue squares on the top. Other defragmentation programs had other visual displays, but the result was always something that looked better organized, giving the user the satisfaction of an optimized hard drive. I never timed a computer to see how much the defragmentation program improved performance, but I believed I noticed the difference and took an odd pleasure in knowing I had cleaned up my hard drive, even though I was often using less than 50% of the available storage space.

Metaphorically speaking, we can think about how humans process information and store memories or mental algorithms the same way. We can imagine our finite brains, like our finite computer hard drives, running programs and storing information, and we can imagine our brains getting cluttered over time in such a way that makes our mental processing suboptimal. As we struggle to recall a word in Spanish, we can imagine our brains searching the fragmented Spanish program in our brain, and we are often surprised to remember the word the next day for no apparent reason. As we grow and mature, we can imagine deleting old software, like the program for Santa Claus and the Easter

Bunny, and replacing them with more scientific ways of thinking that help us detect patterns in reality and make accurate predictions.

Our experiences in the world shape how our hard drives develop over time, but the human organism also shapes the process. In education, for example, people learn in ways that is hard-wired early in our development. We can give the best lecture or make the best Power Point slides, but this is not the best way for people to learn, so we should adjust our education to how we best learn, such as practical exercises. Not to mention, whereas we can save and delete files and programs from a hard-drive, humans are organic, so we cannot delete unwanted programs or memories at will or wipe the slate clean. What we learn and experience at a young age often stays with us our entire life, perhaps below the level of immediate awareness. We can retool or use our software programs in new ways, such as channeling the love we have for our children to our fellow man. Even if we are fortunate enough to be raised in a positive environment that wards off many of the suboptimal traps or dead ends, we are still dealing with an organism that reached evolutionary maturity long before the development of modern states.

As satisfying and interesting this metaphor might be, we should shift to the two reasons it is important for political philosophy. The first point is mental defragmentation (the organic term is pruning) is possible. The human organism naturally grows and matures with time, but it does not naturally reach its full potential with time alone. Activity is required. However, organic change or progress is not like digital progress on a hard drive. If people are raised with certain biases or superstitions, on both sides of the political spectrum, we can transcend them over time, but the process is slow and difficult. For example, the social sciences demonstrate that people living in a state of nature are distrustful of people who act and look different, which results in things like racism and is not limited to any one race. In this sense, racism is "natural" because it exists in all times and in all places. However, given that people living in a state of nature are not living in accordance with their true nature or teleology, they can learn over time to overcome this bias as they learn to expand their horizons beyond their band or tribe. This does not mean everything people think or believe in a state of nature is false, but it means change is possible and often takes time.

In addition to eliminating biases and superstitions, achieving organic growth requires us to push ourselves to new levels of refinement and endurance along the narrow path. If we want to have people in our society who perform brain surgery, conduct symphonies, or write novels, people will have to jump into the furnace of life and transform themselves to achieve mastery. If people sit around the jungle eating bananas and mating all day, they will never spontaneously wake up one day and cure cancer, design a skyscraper, or break the world record for the mile. These skills require a sustained level of performance over time, in a way the builds on the previous progress, and transforms the organism to new levels of performance and endurance. Some people will walk the narrow path with greater ease, due to natural ability or resources, but most people do not achieve world-class excellence in their chosen profession with ease. Thus, although personal progress is real and people can overcome their biases and superstitions, this process is often difficult and our organic hard drives (neural networks) crystallize over time in such a way that makes continuous learning difficult, which brings me to the second point.

Given the many challenges of life—limited abilities, limited resources, limited luck, threats to our safety, etc.—the majority of people will find their hard drives or neural networks crystallizing in suboptimal, Nash equilibrium ways as they grow into adulthood—the bell curve distribution of refinement. I cannot imagine a single person looking back on life and honestly concluding that they had fulfilled 100% of their potential in every way. We all could have done better, given the right circumstances or more effort.

Most of us do our best and carve out whatever niche we can, knowing everyone else is in the same boat. Given that people differ in many ways due to nature and nurture considerations, we have to accept that people will have different interests and will want to live in different ways, which takes us back to the space of liberty. We can pass legislation to nudge people in the right direction, such as saving for retirement, or shape culture, such as public service announcements against drunk driving, but the results will taper off as people reach the natural limits of their mental plasticity. If people like spending time and money listening to country music or gangster rap, playing video poker in a sports bar, or shopping for new shoes and drinking pumpkin-spiced lattes, then we as a society have no business telling them to use their time and money in other ways. Not to mention, many people who chastise people for their simple pleasures often have their own simple pleasures, like abstract art. The important question is whether the person is fulfilling his or her social responsibilities (working, paying taxes, raising children, obeying the law, etc.) and not living parasitically off society as a matter of course.

Unto Caesar

In the New Testament, some opponents of Jesus tried to trick him by asking him about paying taxes to Caesar, probably with hope that Jesus would give the wrong answer and get in trouble with the Romans. Jesus, fully aware they were trying to trick him, looked at a coin with a picture of Caesar and replied with his famous, "Well then, give to Caesar what belongs to Caesar, and give to God what belongs to God." The importance of the passage cannot be stressed enough because it set the stage for the idea of the separation of church and state that shaped Western Civilization. If Jesus had said, "Let us make the realms of Caesar and God one and the same," we would be living in a different world. To the dismay of many revolutionaries, Jesus was in the business of personal salvation, not political reform or land redistribution, although he gave advice about how to live in this world and had harsh words for the corrupt and powerful. Throughout history, there have been conflicts between church and state, with the church sometimes crowning the king or getting involved in affairs of the state, such as fighting wars or Crusades, but the separation was always implicit and has lasted until this day.

Sometimes, the separation was less clear and the relationship was too cozy, like the establishment of the Church of England, but the colonists and the Founding Fathers saw the dangers of this and sought to establish a nation built on religious freedom without an official church, and thus avoiding a situation where the state could dictate which doctrines to believe and fill the ranks of the church as political favors. As should be clear to anyone who has read the U.S. Constitution, there is no separation clause. There is an establishment clause in the First Amendment, which says, "Congress shall make no law respecting an establishment of religion, or prohibiting the free exercise thereof." As the second half of that statement makes clear, nothing suggests the ideas and values of individuals and society should not reflect the religion of the citizens in their personal lives or in government. Some people might not like the establishment clause, but given that the Constitution is the law of the land, it should be used as one of our axioms in a deductive thought process until the First Amendment is amended.

Most religious people in America today accept that the Bible should not be the playbook for running the government. Some voters might consult the Bible before voting and some elected officials might consult the Bible before voting or making decisions, but no one will be forced to make scriptural references or justifications when voting or making decisions, whereas the Supreme Court must use the Constitution when ruling on cases because the only question the Supreme Court should consider is whether something is constitutional. Some elected representatives might consult the Bible before a vote, but they accept that the Bible will not dictate the outcome of the vote (votes do not require a quoted passage in scripture to be valid) and that the side with the most votes will win even if the results are not consistent with the Bible.

Despite this reasonable solution for religion and the political process, some people believe it is not legitimate to consult the Bible as a basis for making decisions because it supposedly violates the separation clause (which does not exist). The idea is if someone's beliefs about marriage are based on the Bible, this is not a valid belief because the Bible does not accept all forms of marriage. On the other hand, some people believe it is legitimate to consult *Das Kapital* by Marx because it is secular and is therefore not a violation of the separation clause (which does not exist). This is an important point. Whereas most of the core beliefs of religious people are metaphysical or theological because they go beyond empirical science, so are most of the core beliefs of Marxists and other political philosophies, and are therefore "religious."

When religious people invoke the Bible to speak out against abortion, based on the belief that life begins at conception, this is not a disqualifying position just because it is grounded in religion and the Bible, for two reasons. First, there is no separation clause in the Constitution, which means people can use the Bible as a basis for voting and can speak about it publicly. If someone invokes scripture before voting on a law, the vote still counts. Second, many of the major issues in political philosophy are metaphysical or theological in the sense that they go beyond sense perception and science. What experiment would we devise to prove we have a right to life, liberty, and the pursuit of happiness? What do we mean when we say all people are equal? Science can tell us about how a fetus develops until viability, but we have to decide when we will treat the fetus as a human with rights.

Unfortunately, this left-right dichotomy is often couched in terms of religious dogmatism versus enlightened secularism, even though both sides are promoting equally metaphysical or theological ideas. The fact that you do not invoke the deity to support your beliefs does not mean your beliefs are scientific or not religious. The doctrine of social justice is not scientific and goes beyond the evidence to the realm of metaphysics or theology. Even though there is no separation clause in the Constitution, the left has done an effective job of convincing unsuspecting people that the separation clause exists and that any political point backed by religious belief is at best not legitimate or at worst bigoted or intolerant. On the flip side, by claiming their ideas are based on science or not based on religion, the left tries to create a false sense of legitimacy because the claim that a fetus is not a human with a right to life is no less of a metaphysical or theological (religious) claim than the claim that a fetus is a human with a right to life. On top of this, many of the beliefs on the left are accepted on faith, without scientific proof, so the beliefs of the left are less secular than many are willing to admit. In short, because the left has been able to couch their beliefs in a context outside of religion, they have been able to sell their points to unsuspecting people and have been able to keep religious people on the defensive.

Turning to liberty, the point should be clear. For policy issues that are grounded in numbers and scientific research, such as measuring the impact of welfare spending or changes to the education curriculum, we should follow the evidence to make rational decisions, assuming the money exists to fund the programs. However, many of the controversial issues in political philosophy lack such clear evidence, which means people will have consult their conscience on the right thing to do. The historical attempts by Marx and others to reduce political philosophy to a science failed for obvious reasons: political philosophy is not science. We should not be slaves to tradition, like stoning people who commit moral offenses, especially after we have made the transition to a modern state, but we should be cautious about believing that thousands of years of human history are null and void and that we can wipe the slate clean. As Hegel warned us, the rational people who are capable of drafting a social contract are the product of a society that is governed by traditions with origins in the darkest depths of history. There is no rational reason to be intrigued by King Arthur removing a sword from a stone, but the story grips us in ways that words on a piece of paper never will.

If a group of people advertises that they live according to the Bible, and these people obey the laws and fulfill their social obligations, we should respect them. Likewise, if another group of people advertises that they live according to *Das Kapital* and share their resources communally, and these people obey the laws and fulfill their social obligations, we should respect them as well. And lest the left dwells too much on the claim that the voter base of the right is not refined or sophisticated, they should remember that the same applies to their voter base—rednecks and welfare queens. The question becomes, if we are going to live in a pluralistic society where people are allowed to live in accordance with liberty, with some people freely exchanging goods and services, some people sharing their goods and services communally, and others living according to other arrangements, then what kind of government do we need (at a local, state, and federal level) to ensure that all these groups have the right to live according to their beliefs?

CONCLUSION

Liberty is one of the defining universals of modern political philosophy. Most people along the political spectrum embrace liberty, which is not as positive as it sounds because the only way for people on the left and the right to agree that liberty is a good thing is to have a different understanding of what it means. Whereas people on the left understand liberty in terms of the government protecting them from big business or exploitation, people on the right understand liberty in terms not being oppressed by the government. Liberty means we have a space in our lives to do as we please, on our own terms, without being coerced or oppressed, to fulfill our own ends as rational people, even if our time, resources, and efforts could be put to better use for the collective whole.

The key to understanding liberty is Kant's idea that humans are ends in themselves. As humans take the narrow path from a social organism to a modern state, liberty grows as people specialize in the complex skills that are required to sustain a modern state. However, the most important goal of this process is helping people live fulfilling lives. Society benefits from people with specialized skills, like medicine or plumbing, but the pursuit of these skills is an end unto itself. People should not be coerced to learn these skills in the name of social progress. This is the fork in the road for political philosophy: you either believe in liberty and measure social progress by how many people have liberty, or you believe society or the state is an end unto itself and that the duty of all people is to subjugate their own liberty to the greater good, without any clear indications of what this greater good is and who defines what it means.

PART III. PARERGA & PARALIMPOMENA

CHAPTER SEVEN. FINAL THOUGHTS

As was the case in *The Political Spectrum*, any attempt to develop a cohesive and consistent philosophical system will inevitably have some gaps or loose ends. A football team can develop a complex system of plays and watch videos to defeat an opponent, but the coaches and players will still have to be prepared to think on their feet and respond to unforeseen circumstances, such that we can all imagine a scenario in which the right play for a particular situation will not be found in the playbook but will be obvious to those who understand the situation. Likewise, there are other topics that are relevant because they help us think about political philosophy in new ways or because they do not fit nicely into one of the earlier chapters.

Two Systems

As Russell and Scruton observed, philosophy exists in a realm between science and theology, just as the ideas in this book exist in the realm between the fleeting world of Heraclitus and the eternal world of Parmenides. Although the findings of science cannot be used to develop a systematic political philosophy, because philosophy is required to explain what makes science possible, philosophy can lean on science to stay on the narrow path. If we espouse a philosophical view of the world, it should be consistent with the findings of science and there should be no contradictions. For example, promoting the traditional family would be an invalid philosophical belief if the evidence proved that children from traditional families on average performed below average and children from broken families on average performed above average. Or, if we espouse something resembling the realism of Aristotle, we can look to science to assess whether universals have a foundation in reality or are merely mental creations.

We can create the concept gold, but whether it has an objective reference in reality requires the tools of science, such as identifying the atomic number or density. However, merely studying empirical reality will not lead us all the way to the idea of realism. For this we need philosophy and the power of the intellect. Therefore, whenever I find a scientific book that shines a bright light on the most important claims of philosophy, I relish the opportunity to throw my own ideas on the butcher block to face the wrath of the cleaver. One such book was Nobel Prize winner Daniel Kahneman's *Thinking, Fast and Slow*, which captures the most important findings in the history of modern psychology. Weighing in at over 400 dense and insightful pages, I enjoyed putting my own ideas through the wringer and coming out the other end with a new perspective.

I could never do justice to the entire book in this brief section, so I will focus on some key points that are relevant to the ideas in this book. The major theme of the book is the human mind operates with two systems, but this should be understood in a metaphorical way. The brain operates as a whole and there are many areas of overlap, so the claim that there are two systems represents a convenient, human way of looking at how the mind works. It does not mean there are two independent networks of neurons that fire separately in parallel in the same way that the digestive system is distinct from the respiratory system. It is more like the difference between slow twitch (Type I) and fast twitch (Type II) muscles; these muscles always exist side by side in the various muscles, but we can think of them as performing unique functions.

According to this model, System 1 in the brain operates automatically, quickly, with minimal effort, and with no sense of voluntary control. On the other hand, System 2 in the brain allocates attention to mental activity that demands effort, like complex computations, and is often associated with the subjective experience of agency, choice, and concentration. Surprisingly, all the activities we associate with the brain can fit into one of these two systems. As I read the book, I saw a parallel with the distinction that is made in philosophy, especially in Kant and Schopenhauer, between understanding, which effortlessly presents the world of perception and intuitive knowledge, and reason, which makes mental abstractions from the world of perception to construct a hierarchical web of concepts or universals for logical or rational thought. That is, although philosophers throughout history did not have the advantage of modern technical equipment to test these theories, such as functional magnetic resonance imaging (fMRI), they generally had good insights about how the mind works.

If we consider System 1, its main function is to maintain and update our model of the world. We share this with other animals and it cannot be turned off. For example, as we make our way through life, we learn to identify friends and enemies and take appropriate action. Humans seem to have fewer instincts in this area, but anyone with a trained ear can learn to detect the type or size of the animal approaching, to know whether they are in danger. We might be correct or we might make errors, but the filters act automatically and reflect the knowledge we have built over time. If we sense danger, such as walking down a dark alley and know something is wrong, we run, with the understanding we might later find out we were wrong. In this sense, System 1 is impulsive and intuitive. When we call on System 1—when System 1 makes a conclusion, because it never turns off—it does not involve logic or mathematics with the certainty of truth. This automatic function can apply to many things in life, such as selecting a political candidate, assessing the odds of a bet, or comparing two objects.

The problem with System 1, especially in an unrefined stage of development, is it falls victim to biases and systematic errors. It can detect simple relations but often has to call on System 2 for assistance when making a decision that goes beyond direct perception. If you find yourself feeling "lucky" or having a "hunch," perhaps with a mystical feeling that you somehow know better than everyone else, you are probably responding to System 1. This does not mean you will always be wrong with System 1, especially if you are an expert on the issue, but if a decision does not have to be made right away and there is time to call on the assistance of System 2, we should always be cautious about rushing to the effortless judgments presented by System 1.

To use a term that is popular today, System 1 is about generating narratives. Normally, outside the realm of storytelling, the term narrative has negative connotations, such as people saying, "You will not accept the facts because they do not fit your narrative." The idea with narratives and the activity of System 1 is we take a collection of complex, interrelated facts and assemble them into an easy to understand package or framework, such as Republicans are greedy or Democrats are lazy. Some of the important findings of modern psychology are that the mind has a propensity to create narratives, that these narratives selectively choose which facts to highlight, and that these narratives are difficult to change once people believe them.

If we consider System 2, it operates within what we normally call reason or the rational mind. One of the most important ways to think about System 2 is how it relates to System 1. On the negative side,

System 2 tends to be lazy (the path of least resistance) and accepting of the spontaneous, intuitive conclusions of System 1, which are often wrong. As a result, System 2 is often an apologist for System 1, as in the case of people who hold strong political beliefs and only later look for ways to rationalize them, rather than holding a cohesive and consistent system of beliefs and submitting to the conclusions that follow necessarily from them. System 2 is often activated when the model (narrative) of System 1 is violated, but given that System 2 is often lazy or unrefined, it often cannot help.

Even if we use System 2 correctly, it is slower and less efficient for routine decisions. On the positive side, however, as we develop System 2 with hard work and discipline—when we construct a cohesive and consistent hierarchical web of universals—we can reprogram System 1 so that our spontaneous intuitions are more frequently correct, what is known as expertise. System 2 follows rules, compares objects, makes choices, and when we develop it to the point of having self-control, we can use it to overcome the impulses of System 1. And whereas System 1 is focused on jumping to conclusions, System 2 serves the important role of doubting and unbelieving, which is often necessary to avoid error. This does not mean System 2 is better or more important than System 1, but System 2 is what we normally talk about when we consider what separates us from other animals, which in everyday parlance means the power of reason.

I previously raised the ideas of resonance and refinement. Whereas resonance refers to System 1 (things resonate with our current narrative of the world) refinement refers to the degree to which System 2 has been developed to shape System 1. This is the dialectical process whereby we develop our understanding of the world by refining our universals. As we develop a valid, hierarchical web of universals, this in turn reshapes and prunes (organic defrag) our tools of intuition so that our intuitions are correct more frequently, which means we can reach true conclusions with less effort. For example, when I studied mathematics, problems that initially took hours to solve would later take only minutes as my brain learned to see through the nonessentials, to recognize the patterns, and take the most efficient path to the correct answer. The same idea goes for chess: great players do not consider every possible combination of moves; they see patterns that allow them to see the best sequence of moves to advance the game toward victory, or even to recognize certain defeat.

In this way, intuition is recognition within associative memory, but recognition of things we have done before many times at the right level of intensity. It does not refer to the recognition of Plato in which we recall the Ideas or Forms we saw before this incarnation. People who do not achieve System 2 refinement, due to not having sufficient cognitive strain, will tend to fall into a pattern of predictable patterns of cognitive biases and errors that manifest themselves in political party stereotypes (red necks or welfare queens). This has important consequences for political philosophy because once people crystallize into this bell curve distribution of refinement, it will be difficult to convince them with rational arguments, and it will be difficult for them to escape the traps and common errors of System 1.

If we consider one of the most important findings of modern psychology—that we are not as rational as we imagine ourselves to be—then we have to consider how this influences the role of government. On the one hand, if we know people will have a difficult time escaping the cognitive traps of an unrefined System 1, often due to circumstances beyond their control, then we have to consider the role of paternalism in government to protect us from ourselves. Some would argue that people should have the right to make decisions, even harmful decisions, but if we can predict with accuracy the errors people will make and the collective damage it could do, does it make sense for the government to interfere? The short answer is yes, because we are already do it with laws and regulations—product safety, investigating scams, and so on—but the long answer is a modified no, for three reasons.

First, while we should promote easy and inexpensive ways to avoid significant problems, such as clean water and clean hands, we have to remember the government is run by people just like us, many of whom have political agendas or have a difficult time escaping the cognitive traps and blind spots of an unrefined System 1. Therefore, it is not always clear whom we could trust to implement paternalism, unless both parties reach consensus because the problem is obvious to all.

Second, if we consider the power of dialectic, making good and bad decisions in many ways is essential to our biological growth and maturity. Within reason, people need to develop and refine their own narrative of successes and failures to grow as humans, just like the butterfly has to struggle to escape the cocoon to survive on the outside. Excessive paternalism could stifle this process and keep people in a stage of dependence, but allowing people to use addictive substances like heroin would be irresponsible. To use a popular term, we can "nudge" people in the right direction by providing incentives, such as providing tax breaks to save for retirement, but we should be careful when interfering with the process of biological growth and maturity.

Third, we should remember that few policies are politically neutral. For example, children who grow up in traditional families and go to church have many advantages in life, are more charitable and better behaved, and avoid many problems in life, so should we "nudge" people toward traditional families and church? Some people would say yes and some people would say no. If our motivating factor were to implement the findings of science, the answer would be yes. The point is, once we open the door to allowing the government to tell us what is best for us, beyond a reasonable degree, there is no objective way to do this that would avoid the problems of political division.

THE RIGHTEOUS MIND

Continuing with the butcher block theme, people who want to hold a serious discussion about political philosophy or have a bright light shined on their ideas to reveal what can stay and what must go should read Jonathan Haidt's splendid book, *The Righteous Mind: Why Good People are Divided by Politics and Religion*. The book addresses the System 1 and System 2 analysis of the previous section, so there is no need to repeat it, but most important for this book, Haidt relies on empirical research, not abstract theories, to develop of theory of political philosophy morals that is consistent with many of our intuitions but with some important surprises that will require most people along the political spectrum to reconsider their core beliefs. To add credibility to Haidt's theory, his conclusions were not consistent with where he began the journey. He began his academic career as a liberal on the left but over time allowed the collection of empirical evidence to change his beliefs by recognizing that morality is more comprehensive than most liberals on the left are aware and that the social conservative argument on the right side of the political spectrum is more complete.

Equally important for this book is his use of the term "moral receptor," which helps explain what teleology means in the context of political philosophy. Haidt's research shows the mind is hard-wired with six moral receptors—care, liberty, fairness, loyalty, authority, and sanctity, which I will address individually below. These moral receptors are neither eternal like the world of Parmenides nor fleeting like the world of Heraclitus. The moral receptors have source code on the root drive that can withstand some tweaking and pruning to fit our particular situations but our morals are grounded in our biology, not in the material world. Haidt analyzes the source code for each moral receptor from an evolutionary perspective, which is more speculative, but the more important point is how the six moral receptors manifest themselves as a matter of fact in a modern state. We are not caring because our material circumstances prompt us to be caring. We are caring because we are hard-wired to care. Changing our diet, work, or the books we read will not add or remove moral receptors. Our diet, work, and the books we read might twist individual moral receptors beyond recognition or suppress others, or we might try to create new ones without a foundation, but if we are property nourished, nurtured, and educated, the six moral receptors will develop in a natural way and shape the way we live. Once we recognize and accept this, the next step is to address them individually and explore whether we should give them equal weighting within political philosophy.

1. *The Care/Harm Foundation.* Despite the human propensity for war and violence, we are hard-wired with a propensity to care for people and avoid harm. From an evolutionary perspective, the origin of this receptor might have been a response to the suffering of our own children, such as a crying baby, which would help the species survive. In a modern state this caring extends beyond the people in own family tree, to include foreigners. If an individual or group is viewed as being harmed in some way, the caring foundation kicks in and motivates us to act in their defense. As Haidt concluded, everyone cares but liberals care more. In fact, the morality of the liberal left is weighed heavily in favor of the care foundation, often at the expense of the others.

2. *The Liberty/Oppression Foundation.* Despite the human propensity to oppress and enslave people, we are also hard-wired to fight back against oppression in the name of liberty. From an evolutionary perspective, the origin of this receptor might have been a visceral response to bullies or tyrants, but in a modern state it manifests itself in how we face restraints to our liberty, including the government. Liberty is often the rally cry of underdogs, victims, or powerless groups, and often operates in tension with the authority/subversion foundation. All people along the political spectrum value liberty, but they value it in different ways. For example, whereas liberals on the left (progressives) promote government action to protect them from oppression, such as from big business, liberals on the right (libertarians) promote restraints on government power. Libertarians value liberty above all else, almost to the exclusion of the other five foundations, and progressive liberals consider it the second most important.

3. *Fairness/Cheating Foundation.* Despite the human propensity to cheat and break the rules, we are also hard-wired to cooperate and play by the rules, with the goal of not getting exploited by free riders. From an evolutionary perspective, the origin of this receptor might

be reciprocal altruism, or tit for tat, which has applications for game theory. Of interest, Haidt's research began with the assumption that fairness meant equality of outcome but additional research indicated fairness is best understood as proportionality. When fairness is understood this way, the left has less interest and the right has more interest. The right understands fairness in terms of the law of karma or the Protestant work ethic—working hard and getting what you deserve, for better or worse. Liberals on the left generally support fairness as proportionality on the positive side but are less supportive of the negative side—rewards, not punishment. In fact, liberals on the left are usually willing to dismiss fairness if it conflicts with caring. Everyone values fairness as proportionality but the right values it more.

As Haidt observed, the split between the first three moral receptors and the next three moral receptors is the key to understanding the difference between progressive liberals and social conservatives, between the left and the right. Whereas progressive liberals put most of their eggs in one basket with the caring receptor and libertarians put most of their eggs in one basket with the liberty receptor, social conservatives give all six moral receptors equal consideration when developing a political philosophy. Some liberals go as far as saying the other three moral receptors should be rejected and have no place in a modern state. Many years ago there was a book about how everything we need to be good adults we learned in kindergarten—be nice, be fair, and do not bully other people, which encapsulates the first three moral receptors. Although platitudes like this sell books and resonate with people on a superficial level, they do not address the more difficult social challenges we face with collective behavior in a modern state. Whereas liberals shift the burden of caring to the government (funded by the rich who pay their "fair" share) and libertarians want to be left alone and not burdened with the problems of others, social conservatives alone expect all people to carry the burden of all six moral receptors. As Haidt argued, ignoring or rejecting any of the six moral receptors, which are hard-wired into us, is a recipe for failure.

4. *Loyalty/Betrayal Foundation.* One of the great themes of mafia movies is loyalty to the family and death for those who betray this trust. Audiences are intrigued with this but many people feel it has no place in a modern state. If someone or an organization does not behave properly, we have an obligation to betray them. From an evolutionary perspective, the loyalty receptor helped us understand which tribe members were team players and which ones were not, which was a matter of survival when interacting with other tribes. In modern language, the loyalty receptor addresses the challenge

of forming and maintaining coalitions, to include rewarding team players and punishing traitors. As much as some people do not like loyalty, social cohesion depends on it. The Democratic Party would not exist without loyalty. Institutions filled with mercenaries for sale to the highest bidder do not perform well over time. Friendships require loyalty, people we can trust with our secrets. On all levels, loyalty holds people together in positive ways, to the exclusion of others, and does not mean we should cover up criminal behavior. When we consider the conflict of nationalism and universalism (open borders) this argument is grounded in the loyalty receptor. This explains why so many liberals were shocked by the election of Trump. Many liberals apparently do not recognize how much our collective prosperity depends on loyalty to Americans at the expense of other nations. This does no mean we have no global responsibilities or can do as we please. Social conservatives understand loyalty to the nation should be restrained and can limit our options for working with other countries, but the alternative is social entropy.

5. *Authority/Subversion Foundation.* If you attend a liberal protest, there is a good chance the participants will speak out against authority and in support of subversion, which horrifies social conservatives to no end. From an evolutionary perspective, the authority receptor is grounded in patterns of appearance and behavior that indicate higher versus lower rank. However, rather than consider authority in terms of power and oppression, authority evolved in response to the adaptive challenge of forging relationships that will benefit us within social hierarchies. Many liberals do not like authority, and their accusations of abuse of authority are often valid, but liberals did not hesitate to treat President Obama with the authority he deserved. Every group admires authority within its own ranks. Not to mention, authority is also bottom up. If we are going to live in a society in which a hierarchy is inevitable, the authority receptor makes us sensitive to rank or status and to signs that other people are behaving properly, given their position. Authority is a two-way street: if we submit to authority, such as judges, we reserve the right to hold them to a high standard; if they fail to live up to that standard, we reserve the right to reject their authority. If people are selected to lead our organization, the authority we grant them will be proportional to their ability to improve the performance of the organization.

6. *Sanctity/Degradation Foundation.* If we consider the culture war in America, many of the key points focus on the sanctity receptor. Liberals believe social conservatives are oppressive white men who worship outdated ideas, and social conservatives believe liberals live in a world where nothing is sacred—life, religion, the flag, the Founding

Fathers, and so on. From an evolutionary perspective, although I am reluctant to accept this reductionist analysis, Haidt argues the sanctity receptor is grounded in the smells, sights, and other sensory patterns that predict the presence of dangerous pathogens in objects or people, what Haidt called the omnivore's dilemma. Fortunately, we have a natural instinct to avoid poisons and harmful substances, but this also supposedly makes it possible for people to invest objects with irrational and extreme value—positive and negative—which are important for binding groups together. If we consider the U.S. flag, whereas many liberals would consider it just a piece of cloth, even a symbol of oppression, they would not be offended if it was disposed of an improper way. The time-space continuum would not be broken if someone tossed a flag into the garbage. The social conservative would respond that a rational person would be offended, because of what the U.S. flag symbolizes, and that the indifference of the liberal would be indicative of a character flaw, someone not fully cognizant of the history or the culture that made their life possible.

The social conservative argument rests on two ideas. First, the six moral receptors are real and hard-wired into our brains; any denial of this is a denial of science because years of research confirm it, from a scientist who began his career as a liberal no less. We can suppress the six receptors, ignore them, or twist them beyond recognition, but they remain and manifest themselves in a natural way if properly nourished. The idea of "transcending" them makes no sense and is doomed to failure. Second, a proper balance of all six receptors is required to develop and sustain society in a way that is consistent with our nature. That is, the six moral receptors move us along the narrow path of social progress. Social conservatives value liberty, but they recognize there is a point where it transforms into egoism—doing what you want with no concern for how it affects those around you. Social conservative also value caring, but they recognize there is a difference between the feeling of caring and doing something tangible that will help people stay on the narrow path. Liberals get points for caring, but this does not mean their methodologies are more effective. In fact, many social conservatives would label the actions of liberals as uncaring to the extent they promote dependency. If we focus less attention on "I" and more attention on "we," the social conservative argument comes into focus.

How Antifragile We Are

One of the biggest challenges in writing this book has been explaining what I mean by teleology in the context of human biological growth and maturity. The reason for this is the word teleology has a long history dating back to Aristotle that has been under attack for most of the modern age, by philosophers and scientists alike. One solution would be to use a different word, but it is difficult to find another word that captures the three most important elements of teleology—biology, purpose, direction—in a way that does not hark back to teleology. Itemizing the incorrect understandings of teleology could fill an entire chapter. Rather than attempt this, however, I will continue to explain what the term means within my theory, one layer at a time.

A great book that helped me better understand teleology was *Antifragile: Things That Gain from Disorder* by Nassim Nicholas Taleb. Of interest, this book contains a section called "The Teleological Fallacy," which Taleb defines as the illusion that you know exactly where you are going, using the example of travel or making plans. However, teleology has nothing to do with knowing where you are going. In fact, if teleology means this, I would prefer to do away with the term. Teleology as I understand it deals with the internal growth of an organism (the internal burn), such as reaching maturity as an adult, not with how the organism moves from place to place. A falling rock does not follow a parabolic path to the ground due to teleology.

The best way to begin is with Taleb's analysis of three important terms: fragile, robust, and antifragile. Fragile means anything that benefits from tranquility or has more downside than upside potential from random events or shocks, such as a crystal wine glass or an organism that do not respond well to stress. A mosquito is fragile within the forces of nature, relative to a human wielding a flyswatter, but it might not be fragile in a different context. The important point is a fragile object does well in the absence of shocks; it benefits from a smooth existence, like selecting government bonds rather than stocks in a world of low inflation. If a crystal wine glass is left in a cabinet and you return 50 years later, it will still be there, unchanged.

Robust, on the other hand, means anything that can withstand significant random events or shocks. Consider a palm tree along the ocean that withstands typhoon winds year after year, or consider a stone castle in the face an enemy with arrows and swords. A robust object does not need the significant random event or shocks for its survival, but it will withstand them more often than not, although palm trees and castles have natural limits. At the end of the day, as long as the resilient object is not destroyed, it will not change much in the face of random events or shocks.

When we shift to antifragile objects, however, the objects have more upside than downside potential from random events or shocks; that is, the objects actually grow from disorder. As Nietzsche would say, what does not kill us makes us stronger. Antifragile object are not fragile because they need stressors to grow and develop (they will die without them), unlike fragile objects that do not need stressors to survive. And unlike robust objects, antifragile objects are often more limited in terms of the random events and shocks they can withstand. The key difference is a robust object does not need stressors to continue existing (an antifragile object does) and can withstand significant stressors (antifragile objects often cannot).

As we consider the meaning of antifragile, it should be clear it applies to political philosophy. Humans, institutions, and societies are all antifragile, which means any attempt to remove natural stressors from our lives will not protect us; on the contrary, the removal of natural stressors will bring about our demise, the same way the butterfly that was cut out of the cocoon could not fly when it was out because it needed the stressors of escaping from the cocoon to develop its muscles. Likewise, this means we should design our institutions and societies such that they can withstand natural stressor and actually grow stronger as a result. If our institutions and societies are excessively fragile or complex, they will collapse when faced with natural stressors.

According to Taleb, the central illusion of modern life, for humans, institutions, and society, which are antifragile, is that randomness is risky and bad, and that we should do everything in our power to eliminate randomness from our lives. If a crystal wine glass can survive in a cupboard without stressors for 50 years, so can we. For example, according to this illusion, rather than have people face the forces of nature and exchange goods and services according to the laws of supply and demand, we should try to give everyone a predictable life that involves working 40 hours a week in exchange for a predictable paycheck. Rather than allow income or diet to fluctuate randomly from week to week as people struggle to survive, the modern thinking is that should have a predictable income and consume three meals a day.

The comfortable way is not always the best way to structure our lives because life and science demonstrate that people thrive on healthy stress, to include random events and shocks, and that we should do everything in our power to ensure all people get the right exposure to healthy stress. The growth and development of our organism depends on it. The same goes for institutions or societies. All group success involves some chaos and randomness, such as a professional sports team seeking out new players, training, or using trial and error with the playbook to make the necessary adjustments to defeat an opponent. Meditating in a cave will not make us great athletes. Taking a month off or not pushing people beyond their natural limits will not help a team win. Granted, not everything in life should be about winning at all costs, and we should avoid the trap of stressing ourselves out gratuitously, but for those areas where we need to succeed, such as defending ourselves from outside threats or creating wealth to sustain our society, we are doing ourselves a disservice if we do no think of ourselves as antifragile and do not push ourselves to our natural limits.

As the saying goes, we practice like we play. If a hockey team practices at 80%, it will never play at 100% during a game, which is why teams often speak of giving 110% during practice so they can play at 100% during a game. If soldiers fire their weapons only under ideal circumstances, they will not succeed in the fog of war. Think about how contestants on reality television talent shows accelerate their improvement week after week when faced with the stress and scrutiny of judges, live audiences, and the knowledge that millions of people are watching them on television. There is a great scene in the movie Crimson Tide when the captain (Gene Hackman) pushes his team and the submarine to the limit, to help them defeat the enemy during a future attack. He was not being a jerk, even though an overweight sailor died during the exercise. The captain knew the sailors would later thank him if they were ever to face the intensity of war, and they would grow to trust and respect him for giving them the experience of success.

In the case of complex systems, like a modern state or a multinational corporation, institutions are weakened if they are deprived of these stressors. Muscles atrophy with time. Skills atrophy with time. For anyone who has had the good fortune of experiencing the thrill of being part of a high performance team, the road is bumpy, involves trial and error, and can be guided by general principles and rules of thumb to keep everyone on the same page. Unfortunately, as institutions or teams grow and mature there is a tendency to make the process smooth and linear and to manage the activities of everyone with a complicated system of rules and regulations, which eat away at the natural strength and spontaneity of the team. A similar thing happens on a macroeconomic level with massive government debt and centralized planning. Modern states benefit from some centralized planning and a rational monetary system, but the more we squeeze the chaos and randomness out of the system and try to replace it with predictability and rules, the more we will squeeze the life out of the system. Depressions and deflation are not good things unto themselves, but many times they are the only way to remove the excesses of monetary expansion and inflation from the system to get the economy back on track. A ship has a rudder to steer the ship, but you might as well let go of the wheel if you steer the ship into a storm with 100-foot waves.

A key point about antifragile in the context of political philosophy has to do with the topic of welfare. The left and the right go back and forth on this topic, with the left calling the right heartless for not wanting to help people with welfare and the right calling the left heartless for wanting to addict people to welfare and kill their incentive to work. The important points to remember are that 1. a modern state needs a welfare system to address the inevitable shocks that occur in a capitalistic system (think of it as insurance to protect us from unforeseen events), and 2. any person who receives welfare payments should view themselves as being in an unfortunate situation that should be rectified as soon as possible. They should not view themselves as entitled and comfortable for the indefinite future. To quote Ben Franklin:

> I think the best way of doing good to the poor, is not making them easy in poverty, but leading or driving them out of it. I observed... that the more public provisions were made for the poor, the less they provided for themselves, and of course became poorer. And, on the contrary, the less was done for them, the more they did for themselves, and became richer.

We can agree or disagree as to whether the empirical data support this claim (Do people stop applying for jobs while welfare benefits continue and begin applying for jobs when welfare benefits end?), but the spirit of the quote is important. What should be obvious is people should not aspire to become welfare recipients and should aspire to stop receiving welfare benefits as soon as possible by returning to the labor force, for their own good and for the good of society.

I am not suggesting Democrats have a conscious plan to grow the welfare recipient population to expand their voter base, but Democrats shy away from language or policies designed to nudge people in the uncomfortable direction of ending their dependency on welfare benefits. Republicans often overstate how much money goes to welfare payments, as a percentage of GDP, but this should be offset with how much wealth is not added to the economy by the people who are not working. (If a person used to make $15 per hour and now collects $10 per hour in welfare, the net drain on the economy is $25 per hour, not $10.) Some incentives exist to keep people on welfare or avoid returning to the workforce, for fear of losing welfare benefits. Why work longer and harder for the same or less pay? Many people who receive welfare benefits face many of the stresses that are required to keep them on the path of growth and maturity, to keep them antifragile, but we are doing a disservice to people if the system is structured to keep them dependent on the system rather than making the system depend on them. Once we agree on this theoretical point, we can review the numbers to see where we are in terms of providing people the right incentives to avoid long-term dependency.

PERPETUAL REVOLUTION (NASH EQUILIBRIUM PART II)

I previously analyzed dialectic and how it applies to the narrow path of social progress and political philosophy. The idea was people in a society can use a process of trial and error over time to see what works and what does not work. However, whereas trial and error often begins from nothing and has no particular destination in mind, such as children making up rules for a new game, in many cases, such as political philosophy, dialectic is a process of trial and error to arrive at a natural destination—the truth. We hope to arrive at the right destination but we do not have enough information at the beginning to map out narrow path.

People on the left and the right have a vision for how society should be, and both sides believe society will arrive at something true and beneficial if their vision is fulfilled. There are limiting variables, however, which shape the dialectical process and often leave us with suboptimal results. For example, if a country has one natural resource, such as oil, the exploitation and management of this natural resource will shape the dialectical history of the country, for better or worse. A country with large oil reserves would be wise to exploit and manage them rationally, but the resources required to manage the natural resource will be at the expense of other economic activities (opportunity cost), and success in this business activity will depend on the global price of oil. If we factor in the most important variables— culture, demographics, geography, climate, and so on—the potential narrow paths for social progress are more limited than most are willing to admit. For example, consider how Panama's history was a function of geography and the building of the Canal. We can consider the single commodity economies (oil or mining) of Africa to see that external factors often shape and limit social progress.

If we combine the historical reality of ongoing social change with ongoing attempts to establish social stability, we should not be surprised that revolutions play an important and sometimes inevitable role in history, such as the French and American Revolutions. Historians and social scientists have theories about how and why revolutions occur, but this section will focus on the type of government we have to identify limiting factors and provide ammunition to discredit the pursuit of Utopia.

Aristotle had an effective model for thinking about social progress and political philosophy that is useful today. If we consider the possible types of government, there are three convenient categories: rule by one, rule by few, or rule by many, each with a correct and corrupt version. If we consider one of the frustrations of politics today—gridlock—many people might admit it would be a welcome change if we could have a wise, enlightened monarch to make decisions with the country's best interests in mind, without the drama, gridlock, and compromise that defines politics today. Who would not want a leader to cut pork from the budget by decree and enforce the laws equally for all people, without being burdened by political parties or the other branches of government? Granted, checks and balances can be good, but if we had a humble and selfless ruler who always does the right thing and for the right reasons, we would never have to worry about many of the problems we see in the news today. As much as we can dream, however, such leaders are rare; and if we were to grant power and authority to a monarch, one whose role has real power, not symbolic, we would probably live to regret it and eventually find ourselves ruled by a tyrant, the corrupt version of monarchy. If you create a position of power, people who seek power for the wrong reasons will pursue it.

If we consider the next option, rule by few, the same idea applies and is often called aristocracy. In an ideal world, if we could identify a small group of wise and enlightened individuals to rule, we would potentially have the same benefits of being ruled by the enlightened leader, with the added benefit of having multiple viewpoints, like a council of elders. However, the same problem arises, to include the process of selecting them and deciding whether or not their power and status would transfer to their children, who would probably be groomed from a young age to rule. If we give power to a small group of people, then corruption will slowly permeate the system, in which case we will find ourselves ruled by an oligarchy, the corrupt version of aristocracy.

Finally, we have rule by many, what Aristotle called polity, which is prominent around the world today and is defined by electing "many" representatives to rule and make decisions on our behalf. Each society must define "many" but the key idea is no individual or small group should control the government. One of the best ways to distribute power to avoid the abuse of power is to establish multiple branches of government with checks and balances. The inevitable result, however, in a country with 330 million people, 435 congressmen, and

100 senators, is gridlock and compromise. Social progress along the narrow path in this political reality is difficult because the system is based on compromise, which means we will probably fall short of our dreams, but the benefit is we will avoid the excesses of tyranny and oligarchy. Just as rule of one and rule of few have good and bad versions, the concern with polity is it will transform into rule of all, what the Greeks derogatorily called democracy, the corrupt version of polity. This makes strategic planning and rational decision making difficult because every decision the government makes depends on the whims of the voters from day to day.

	Correct	Corrupt
One Ruler	Monarchy	Tyranny
Few Rulers	Aristocracy	Oligarchy
Many Rulers	Polity	Democracy

Political philosophers often theorize about how societies transition from one location on the chart to the next. For example, history shows transitions from top to bottom, such as monarchy changing to aristocracy or aristocracy changing to polity. Or, some governments integrate all three options, such as having a king (one ruler), an upper house (few rulers), and a lower house (many rulers). Likewise, history shows transitions from left to right, such as monarchy decaying into tyranny, aristocracy decaying into oligarchy, or polity decaying into democracy. Of interest, Aristotle spoke positively about monarchy but recognized the corrupt form of monarchy, tyranny, was the worst form of government that should be avoided. Aristocracy was not as good as monarchy, but the corrupt form of aristocracy, oligarchy, was less bad than tyranny. Finally, Polity was not as good as aristocracy, but the corrupt form of polity, democracy, was less bad than oligarchy, which suggests Aristotle considered polity what we today would call the Nash equilibrium destination of social dialectic to avoid the abuses of tyranny and oligarchy. Polity has flaws, but it requires us to hold the line with discipline to avoid slipping into democracy. Aristotle stressed the importance of avoiding democracy because he argued the resulting chaos would set the stage for a takeover by a tyrant or an oligarchy that promised to restore law and order, and the social revolution continues. Modern political philosophy is more complex than this simple model, but it serves the purpose of helping us think about political systems in the context of Nash equilibrium.

As Winston Churchill quipped, democracy (representative government or polity) was the worst form of government—except for all the others. We reach the destination of modern state polity by combining the narrow path of social progress with the Nash equilibrium path of least resistance to reach a sustainable equilibrium that helps us avoid perpetual revolution or violence. Polity is suboptimal due to gridlock and compromise, but the net benefit of a stable polity is we avoid the excesses of tyranny and oligarchy and create an environment in which individuals are free to pursue their own biological growth and maturity along the narrow path. No one disagrees that sports teams, companies, or institutions benefit from strong leadership and centralized control, assuming we want the best results, but the same idea does not apply to society; we can quit a sports team if we do not like the coach but we cannot quite society. If a coach goes over the edge, he gets fired; but if the government goes over the edge, we all suffer. There are two reasons most people are willing to support the suboptimal system of representative government: first, the dangers of tyranny and oligarchy should be avoided at all costs; and second, representative government with liberty is the best way to ensure people have the best opportunity to fulfill their own teleology along the narrow path.

Our political system might be suboptimal, but our individual lives do not have to be. Individuals can reach their full potential in a society that is suboptimal. People on the left are correct to recognize that state intervention is required to achieve many of their social objectives or their vision of Utopia, which results in a corresponding reduction in liberty. We could use the power of the state to achieve many social objectives that we could not achieve with voluntary action or with people left to their own devices, such as banning smoking to improve the health of society, lowering the speed limit to 45 mph to reduce traffic deaths, or prohibiting opioid pain killers to reduce addiction, but many thoughtful and intelligent social conservatives would argue that the vision of the left is not a worthy pursuit and would invite the abuse of power.

GLOBALISM

One of the most contentious ideas today in political philosophy is globalism, which includes contentious policy issues like free trade, open borders, and one world government. Whereas self-proclaimed elites and their acolytes with a natural bent for globalism usually promote the idea, many working-class citizens of individual countries who are facing the real consequences of globalism, such as lost jobs, are more skeptical and have voted with their feet, evidenced by the Brexit vote for the United Kingdom to leave the European Union and the election of Donald Trump. If Europe is unable to form a political unity (a single currency does not a political unity make), what hope or possibility is there for globalism or a one world government that includes diverse places like Europe, Latin America, Africa, and Asia? Do we really think all the countries in the world will ever cede sovereignty to a one world government? Could this one world government be trusted to protect our interests? How would this government be selected? What mechanism would we have to remove them from office if we are not satisfied with their performance?

The idea of countries establishing a forum like the United Nations (UN) to discuss or arbitrate issues of mutual interest or to establish global objectives, such as stopping human trafficking or helping refugees, has merit, but most countries will reserve to the right to opt out of some issues or invoke veto authority for other issues. Some issues should be raised at a global level, such as managing international air lanes and maritime shipping routes, so the basic idea of globalism or a one world government-like institution makes sense.

With this introduction out of the way, we should consider the more contentious issues that will demonstrate why anything resembling globalism or one world government is not in the cards and would be a bad idea. As is always the case with political philosophy, we will begin our discussion at a fundamental level to situate the problem. If we consider globalism or one world government, the flip side of this is ceding national borders and sovereignty. They are mutually exclusive. Otherwise, if countries are allowed to defend their borders from outsiders and to act in their own self-interest, often in a way that offsets the zero-sum interests of other countries, then globalism or one world government would not be possible. The state or government should possess a monopoly on coercion within a defined geographic area or we can hardly consider it a state or government, with one caveat I will address soon enough.

To show why this is true, consider my home state of Minnesota. What if Minnesota were to mint its own money, withhold taxes from the federal government, raise a military, and establish border crossing points to stop other American citizens from entering the state freely? What if Minnesota were to engage in an aggressive trade and security agenda that was at odds with the interests of other states or the United States of America as a whole? In this scenario, people would rightly conclude that Minnesota was no longer part of the Unites States of America, just as any country that maintained its full sovereignty and borders could never be part of a one world government. As it stands, the United States of America is a republic; the states wield significant authority, per the 10th Amendment of the Constitution, but the states do not have the right to mint their own money, withhold taxes from the federal government, raise a military, or establish border control points. Thus, when we think about the move toward globalism or one world government, we should do so by tracking the degree to which individual nations have or do not have enforceable borders and sovereignty.

If we consider the basic building block of life, the cell, we see an organism that defends its borders and takes steps to survive. If a cell were to open its borders and allow other entities to enter and disrupt the internal processes of the cell, the cell would not live long to tell the story. The same goes for an organism composed of cells, like an animal or a human. If we were to make cuts in our skin to allow outside entities (virus, bacteria, etc.) to enter and disrupt our internal processes, we would not live long to tell the story. The same, though to a lesser extent, applies to families. If a family were to unlock its doors and welcome all outsiders, the family would soon find itself with an empty home without any food, or even worse, the victim of crime. The family might allow family or friends to come and go as they please, perhaps to borrow a cup of sugar, but the home will soon cease to be a home if some reasonable measures are not taken to protect the sovereignty of the home, such as walls, doors, and locks.

This analysis could continue as we expand our concentric rings—neighborhood, city, county, state, country, planet, etc. The same logic applies to companies or institutions. Imagine if Apple, Exxon, or Harvard University lacked the authority to protect themselves from outsiders, such that anyone could enter, claim to be an employee or a student, or help themselves to the products or books. Even the most radical left-wing college professor could not hold this point consistently, unless he was willing to face the end of the university and his job. The obvious fact is for any entity or organism to have identity or possess the ability to sustain its own existence, there must be a way to defend borders and maintain sovereignty, especially if we want to avoid the dilution of achievement. Consider an orchestra. What makes the performances great is the orchestra has a mechanism to control who gets in and what they do on the inside. If an orchestra were forced to make room for any person off the street who felt motivated to play or tinker with the instruments, then the orchestra would eventually cease to exist, mostly because people would stop paying money to hear them perform.

This analysis should suffice to show that anything resembling globalism or a one world government will not happen any time in the near future (the trend is reversing). Countries with long histories and strong national identities should not give up the benefits of nationhood for the nebulous goal of globalism or one world government, which does not promise any tangible benefits. Not to mention, if we were to move toward open borders or one world government, the wealth of the developed countries would be diluted to a degree that would be unacceptable to these countries and limit their ability to provide aid to poor countries. We would not have the Gates Foundation if Bill Gates had not succeeded in the cutthroat world of business to make billions, just as USAID would not have billions in aid to offer developing countries without the tax base of the country. One exception to this rule is if governments are oppressing or exploiting their own citizens in ways that are not consistent with the values of modern states. In this sense, it is legitimate for international institutions like the UN to raise awareness of the actions of authoritarian governments and use the levers of diplomacy to promote the rule of law.

Falling short of a one world government, however, we still have to consider a real situation, namely, open borders. Even if we agree that a full-blown one world government is not possible, there are many people (all on the left) who believe developed countries are morally obligated 1. to allow people from developing countries to live and work in their countries without restrictions, and 2. to not demand that they assimilate the values and culture of the developed country. In fact, the expectation is that the developed country host should assimilate the values and culture of the immigrants in the name of multiculturalism. Ironically, the success of strict border enforcement has made the open borders position seem viable. If we were to open our borders and tens or hundreds of millions of people flooded into our country, even the most left-wing liberals would probably complain and demand tighter border security.

As I discussed previously, the dynamic interaction of cultures can be positive if we learn to learn from each other (America is a nation of immigrants with a set of values that has stood the test of time), but for a particular culture to exist and survive within a border, the culture must be held together by a cohesive and consistent set of values. People who have the good fortune of living in developed countries should be thankful and help the less fortunate, for sure, but it is not clear why a sovereign nation should be obligated to open its borders.

Returning to the idea of cohesive and consistent values, consider a sports team. Most sports have different ways of running the defense, such as zone or man-to-man coverage. Although different strategies have been used successfully in different ways, the important point is whatever strategy is selected has to be used cohesively and consistently to work. If a team were to implement a chaotic mixture of zone and man-to-man coverage, without any rules or principles to guide the process, the team will lose. Different coaches might favor one over the other, depending on the strengths or weaknesses of the players and the opponent, but each strategy works according to its own internal rules or logic and cannot be mixed with others. In this context, not only would a team suffer if it were forced to accept a complete stranger into its ranks, it would also suffer if an existing team member started playing by a different set of rules, like switching from zone to man-to-man coverage without telling anyone. The same logic would apply in many other areas: a business that decides to transition to just-in-time inventory, an infantry unit that decides to employ the phalanx formation, a philosopher who decides to understand the world through the prism of existentialism, a traditional family that decides to live according to the New Testament, and the list goes on and on.

The point is that although we can say one system or strategy is better than the others, there are benefits for sticking to a cohesive and consistent system to achieve our objectives. In some cases, a player will have to use an admittedly inferior system to play because he lacks the skills or refinement to play like a professional, evidenced by how beginning golfers use forgiving equipment and simple swing techniques that are effective on a statistical basis but are incapable of making the big shots. In my case, when I made the transition to a more refined grip, my golf game suffered briefly, but the shift eventually allowed me to improve my game. The risk of pulling people out of their system is two-fold: first, many people will have a difficult time making the transition and end up in a worse situation; and second, it is not clear who we could trust to tell us which new system to implement, given the disagreements among experts. If the data showed that religious people are better citizens (it does), would the experts implement a policy of shifting the population toward religious belief?

I have lived and worked in many countries, rich and poor, and almost without exception the people are rightly proud of their national identity and history and reject the idea of allowing foreigners to live and work in their country without going through a legal process or without learning the language and assimilating the local culture. Some countries are forward leaning with refugees and legal immigrants, but not open borders. Most people have the common sense to recognize that good jobs are a limited resource and that we are only one misunderstanding away from the breakdown of civility, as evidenced by the two world wars of the twentieth century. Most people also agree that global institutions like the UN have a positive role to play in the right circumstances, but if we consider the challenges faced by the European Union, the problems would be compound on a global scale. Society is complex and held together by hundreds or thousands of years of values and traditions in the form of human history. We should resist the temptation to think we know better than our ancestors and can simply wipe the slate clean to rewrite the rules of human nature.

IDENTITY POLITICS

One of the best ways to judge or characterize the political philosophy of an individual or group is to look for inconsistencies. Of course, the idea of looking for inconsistencies makes sense only if we have an objective standard from which to judge. A productive way to counter someone in a debate is to say, "Interesting, but if you are going to be consistent, then you should believe [X]." For example, some people claim it is inconsistent to oppose abortion but to support the death penalty. If people have a right to life and life is sacred, the argument goes, then how can someone be opposed to abortion if they support the death penalty? One way to respond to this criticism is to point out the inconsistency of the argument: well, if you are opposed to the death penalty because people have a right to life and life is sacred, then why do you support abortion? If possible innocence means we should err on the side of caution, how can we allow abortion? An even better way to respond to this criticism would be to dissolve the apparent inconsistency: you cannot make a moral equivalency between an innocent fetus and an adult who has committed a heinous crime.

I am not making an argument for or against the death penalty—I recognize that errors have been made in the judicial system and that some crimes are so heinous as to merit death—but whereas the criminal did something to deserve death, the fetus did not. "But wait," someone might interject, "you cannot make a moral equivalency between an undeveloped fetus and mature human being." Fair enough, I would say, but then the person has just admitted that the fundamental issue surrounding the abortion debate is whether the fetus is a human being, not whether the mother of the fetus has a right to choose—life trumps choice. In other words, the argument that justifies abortion is based on the claim that a fetus is not a human being. After all, if a fetus is a human being, how can a woman have a "right to choose" to kill it?

Continuing with the theme of consistency (we will get to the identity politics point soon enough), the left has been constructive in political philosophy by promoting the idea that each citizen should have the same rights as all other citizens. The Founding Fathers enshrined this idea in the Constitution and the Declaration of Independence ("We hold these truths to be self-evident, that all men are created equal..."), but full membership benefits initially applied to white men over the age of 21 who owned land. Historically, Republican President Lincoln promoted the abolition of slavery via the 13th Amendment and Republican President Eisenhower promoted the first civil rights legislation via the Civil Rights Act of 1957, but the left has done a good job of holding the country's feet to the fire to continue promoting these ideas.

That is why the rise of identity politics from the left has been such an unwelcome development. For a party that has dedicated so much time and effort attacking white male identity politics, the promotion of identity politics for every other group—women, African Americans, LGBT, etc.—is unfortunate. Rather than recognize the dangers of identity politics and defeat it by promoting equal rights, regardless of the superficial labels of identity politics, many on the left have opted to embrace it and proclaim if through megaphones. There is nothing wrong with highlighting that a right to vote should apply to all citizens, regardless of race or gender, but there is something wrong with promoting the idea that people should define themselves by the superficial labels in a way that ends up dividing us. If people think of themselves primarily as women, African American, LGBT, or as being offended, and only secondarily as citizens of the United States of America, it will make consensus more difficult to achieve. The unwillingness of people to reject identity politics indicates they have no interest in equal rights, in the sense of holding all people to the same standard with no privileges. In fact, feminist theory is premised on the idea that power is a key variable in any society, and that by playing on the heartstrings of people with pleas for equality, they are playing a power game in a way that grants special benefits and privileges to their members.

The biggest problem with identity politics is it turns people inward rather than outward for superficial reasons ("I," not "we") and allows a group of people to use their size or volume to receive unfair benefits, often from the government, which means taking finite resources provided by the taxpayers. Granted, if a group's rights are denied, this should be remedied, but as it stands, all rights (not entitlements) already apply to all people equally, and we can continue to rectify historical injustices without resorting to identity politics. For example, there are no laws or regulation to prevent African Americans from registering to vote or going to public school. This does not mean all people have the same opportunities or advantages in society, such as a rich CEO hiring his spoiled son to a senior position despite having more qualified candidates to choose from, but it does mean these opportunities or advantages do not have a legal basis.

When we shift from identity politics to tribalism, we see another way for people to work together in a collective, beneficial way but in a way that does not involve leveraging the government. As I addressed in *The Political Spectrum*, tribalism is a natural stage in the development of any society and there are elements within tribalism that limit the ability of a society to make the transition to a modern state, which is why breaking down the power of tribes is one of the biggest challenges of a modern state. That said, given that science confirms the strongest bonds among people are blood and family, the modern state has to allow tribal bonds to exist at some level because these tribal or family bonds provide the altruistic love people need to reach their potential.

As the saying goes, it's not what you know, it's who you know. Having the right connections is often more important than having the right credentials for getting a good job. Attending an Ivy League school does not mean you are in "the club." Getting a 4.0 GPA is not a fast track to the 1%. People from wealthy networks are likely to "pick their own," just as racial or ethnic groups are likely to "pick their own." For example, Jews, Lebanese, and Chinese succeed in many countries outside their native countries because they have strong communities. Outside the government, some groups leverage their racial or ethnic identities to pool their resources and work together, which often includes "keeping it in the family" for education, marriage, and business. However, as these groups know, their success depends primarily on the values they live by and inculcate in their members, such as conservative values like marriage, religion, sobriety, and a work ethic. They often sustain this success from one generation to the next, but they do so within the group and often without any assistance from the government.

With this in mind, one way to address the challenges of African Americans would be to introduce these values because the default position for the past several decades has been government programs and outside intervention. To promote real change, wealthy and influential African Americans should assume leadership roles by investing in their communities, such as the best and the brightest taking teaching jobs or opening banks or businesses dedicated to promoting economic growth for African American communities. The government can play an active role, but given that the secret of success for this model is the community working together with traditional values, not government assistance, the African American communities should transform from within, to include providing opportunities for each other, such as providing loans for homes or businesses and reducing the number of children born out of wedlock.

As a general rule, the left turns to the state too frequently to address social problems and rarely turns to the trial and error of culture and civil society that show us over time what does and does not work, both in terms of getting results and managing conflicts among people. The state has a role to play in shaping how people behave, but the state and society are not the same thing and people will behave the way they should only if they have a foundation of strong values that promotes the behavior. The state can offer a good school to a child, but the child will struggle to succeed if he lives in a home plagued with poverty and substance abuse. In an ideal world, people will get along and behave because they have shared values, but this means choosing some values over others, even if the values have some quirks and do not work 100% of the time. Working hard in school and getting an accounting job is not "selling out." We would all like to live in a world where each person has an equal opportunity to succeed and where no one gets special favors, but the best opportunities many people have come from their "tribe" (family, community, ethnicity, social networks, etc.), not from the state. If white men are successful, it is not because the state gives them unfair privileges; it is because they were fortunate enough to be raised in families and communities that set them up for success, and the state cannot provide this. Thus, whereas the left is almost right in terms of understanding the power of groups (identity politics), they are wrong in terms of leveraging the real benefits of the group. Rather than unite to influence the state, they would be better served by uniting to promote the benefits of the "tribe" within society.

OBJECTIVITY

One of the biggest challenges in political philosophy is stepping outside of our own skin to analyze important issues objectively in the realm of universals and mathematics, to make the difficult yet intellectually satisfying transition from the self-absorbed, solipsistic "I" to the self-aware, rational "we." Today, unfortunately, we seem to take it for granted and even accept or celebrate the fact that people lack objectivity. In the case of identity politics, we have reached the point where people will vote or are expected to vote for issues based on the various groups or subgroups they belong to, even if the vote is not good in objective ways. How many times have we heard television journalists say something along the lines, "As a female congressional candidate, she will obviously do her best to promote reproductive rights and wage equality." People who would vote for issues because of their gender, race, age, and so on (because they belong to that particular gender, race, age, and so on) of course have no business running for higher office or making decisions for the country. If legitimate wage equality can be proven to exist, then all people should take steps to rectify it, regardless of race or gender.

Our political system benefits from having a genuine diversity of representation (intellectual and professional background, job skills and talents, and so on), to ensure all the important issues are analyzed from a variety of perspectives. At the end of the day, however, we should expect our elected leaders to vote for what is good for their constituents and the country, not their own particular interests. After all, we have the dreaded white men to thank for the abolition of slavery and civil rights legislation. Regarding wage inequality, if someone presents the relevant facts about salaries (industry, position, experience, regular hours worked, overtime hours worked, academic specialization or certifications, historical success for corporate profits, and so on) and makes recommendations to remedy any problems, this is a perfectly reasonable course of action. However, given that companies are desperate for talent and employees often jump from one company to another, the notion that women are systematically underpaid and can do nothing about their predicament, such as going to a company that will offer them a better salary, does not mesh well with the facts. Likewise, if conservatives are going to complain about welfare queens, they have to provide specific facts about how many people are receiving welfare payments, how much they are receiving, and the degree to which the welfare programs diminish the incentive to work, such as by measuring how many people apply for jobs after benefits end. Merely complaining about welfare recipients is not an argument because every modern state needs a welfare system.

One of the most difficult challenges with striving for objectivity, especially as it relates to assessing people on the other side of the political spectrum, is getting beyond perceived motivations. Even though assessing motivations is usually important in life, in the case of political philosophy motivations many times do not matter because we will judge all arguments based on the merits. People on both sides of the political spectrum often construct arguments to support their own personal or selfish interests, such as the banana republic oligarch who promotes "capitalism" when selling products from the monopoly he controls or the revolutionary socialist who nationalizes the energy sector "for the workers" to siphon money into his Swiss bank account, but the high standards of political philosophy demand that we raise the bar and focus on whether the argument is valid. The oligarch might be right to promote capitalism and the revolutionary socialist might be right to nationalize an energy company, even if they have selfish motivations, as long as we take steps to prevent them from abusing their power or personally benefiting from their decisions.

To raise a topic for this book, consider voter ID laws. The left often accuses the right of promoting voter ID laws to make it difficult for minorities to vote, and thus help Republicans win elections, and the right often accuses the left of fighting voter ID laws to allow non-U.S. citizens to vote (or dead people, double voting, etc.), and thus help Democrats win elections. There is evidence that voting decreases when strict voter ID laws are enacted, and there is evidence that non-U.S. citizens vote. Neither side is completely irrational regarding their fears about the intentions of other side. From an objective standpoint, however, the question remains: is it reasonable to expect voters to prove they are eligible to vote, such as proving they are U.S. citizens, as required by the Constitution? Voting is a right for U.S. citizens 18 and older, at least for those who have not lost the right to vote. Given the clear and reasonable restriction that only U.S. citizens are allowed to vote, combined with the fact that many people living in the country (legally or illegally) are not U.S. citizens, there should be a mechanism to prevent non-citizens from voting, as is the case with every country in the world. It does not matter how much evidence exists or does not exist to prove whether voter fraud exits or is rampant. At a minimum, strict enforcement of voter laws would act as a deterrent.

If the good folks on the left are genuinely concerned that minorities are suffering from voter ID laws, they should channel this concern into outreach to ensure everyone has a valid ID and registers to vote, such as raising money for people who cannot afford to pay. They could even propose legislation to provide free IDs and voter registration assistance, although my guess is many minorities might be offended by the idea they are not capable of doing this on their own. Of interest, people on the left do not seem to be losing any sleep for all the other scenarios that require valid ID to prove citizenship—applying for a job, applying for a passport, and so on. It is hard to imagine anyone surviving in today's economy without a valid ID, so outreach would have a positive impact for everyone involved. By a conservative estimate, there are over 20 million people in the country who are not eligible to vote (illegal immigrants, legal workers, green card holders, and others) and that many elections are decided by hundreds or thousands of votes. Therefore, it is not irrational or racist to ensure that only U.S. citizens are allowed to vote and that people who are not eligible to vote have no mechanism to vote.

Along the same lines, we should consider immigration. I am always amazed by how so-called experts who debate this issue in the media deliberately ignore the fundamental difference between legal and illegal immigration, on both sides of the political spectrum. On the one hand, people on the left widely turn a blind eye to illegal immigration because they believe they are being compassionate and undoubtedly assess it will help their voter base, but they conveniently ignore the fact that it is illegal and exposes the illegal immigrants to exploitation (human traffickers, employers, etc.). On the other hand, many business owners on the right turn a blind eye to illegal immigration because their businesses depend on the cheap labor.

Every country should have a rational immigration policy (refugees are a separate issue that should not be conflated with immigration) that is designed to achieve a variety of objectives, such as filling gaps in the workforce. If people on the left truly want to help these people, they should lobby the State Department to offer more work visas to legalize their status, with the understanding that this would be for a limited time and would not be a path to citizenship. If people on the right truly want to reduce the number of illegal immigrants, in addition to enforcing border security, they should demand that businesses request visas for every worker they hire. If there are not jobs for illegals, then people will be less likely to enter the country illegally. They might have to pay them more money and some of those costs will undoubtedly be passed onto the consumer, but the alternative of wage exploitation has no place in our country. Businesses should not be allowed to circumvent immigration law to boost profits. Given that groups on both sides of the political spectrum have a vested interest in perpetuating the problem, we should not expect a solution in the near future.

In addition to focusing on facts, not perceived motivations, another way to achieve objectivity is by assessing something in itself as opposed to how it stacks up relative to other things. If we consider that most people, today and throughout history, have lived in poverty, there are many people living in the United States of America who are living well by historical standards, yet complain because other people are achieving millionaire status. For example, consider the number of people with smart phones, flat screen television, nice cars, daily lattes, and annual vacations, things the elite only 100 years ago could never have imagined. If we consider how the Industrial Revolution and capitalism created the largest and most dynamic economies the world has ever seen, the standard of living most Americans have achieved is impressive. A hard-working person with a high school diploma and a high demand job skill can live a dignified life with a roof over his head and three meals a day for his family. In fact, if we consider other countries, we see people with better academic credentials who work longer hours but with a lower quality of life. There are many countries where people who are middle class by our standards are the ruling elite in their own country, and people who would be lucky to get a civil service job in our country serve as senators or ministers in their own countries. Many foreigners who are in the top 10% of their own country with relatively modest living standards would opt to not live in the United States because they would be in the bottom 50%.

The social pyramid is a zero-sum game; if someone enters the top 1%, someone gets bumped off the list, just like there are only 10 sports teams on the top 10 list. The good news is the zero-sum social pyramid is a social construct and there is no need for us to dwell on our position in the social pyramid, even if the irrational side of us demands that we do. We should learn to achieve objectivity and to assess our success on its own merits, without looking to our left and right or up and down. One of the best ways to do this is to visit a poor country where medical doctors live in what we would consider poverty, such as Cuba. The good news is in an economy focused on creating wealth, the quality of life of everyone can rise, even if our relative position on the social pyramid does not improve, just like everyone benefits when the stock market rises because it is not a zero-sum game. Some people will outperform others and we should ensure people are not allowed to rig the game in their favor, which requires the power of government, but the miracle of wealth creation is not a zero-sum game. There might be social justice explanations for why moving up the social pyramid is so difficult (beyond the challenges of the zero-sum system), but we also have to remember wealthy families give their children the tools they need to succeed, which makes it more difficult to knock them off their position in the social pyramid. If children are immersed in the benefits of wealth (diet, education, activities, etc.), there is a good chance they will be in a better position to assume one of the coveted positions in the top 1%, with the understanding the positions in the top 1% require a high degree of complexity and refinement that often takes years of intense training and preparation. If we look closer, we see that although children benefit from wealth, they benefit from the fact that their parents or grandparents paid it forward, which is created the wealth and made the virtuous circle possible.

CONCLUSION

Truth in advertising: my book presents an argument for a moderate social conservative political philosophy, and by moderate I mean I am right of center and there are many conservatives who would argue that my arguments are not conservative enough. I have no illusions that some conservatives will accept my arguments with limited criticism and some on the left will reject my arguments with unfair criticism, but my hope is that all people along the political spectrum will give me some credit for attempting to support my outlook with well-reasoned arguments that are not self-serving, or for showing new ways to evaluate our arguments, such as thinking in terms of universals and teleology. That said, although I am mostly satisfied with my effort in this book, I recognize that critics could identify some gaps or inconsistencies in my arguments. As someone who values the pursuit of truth, I recognize we all have some blind spots and biases, so I will take this opportunity to shoot some holes in my own arguments.

First, I imagine many readers would argue this book is not inspirational or hopeful enough, not something Tony Robbins would quote during a weekend retreat. Where is the idea of helping every child reach his or her potential? Where is the idea of people around the world living in peace and harmony? After all, if we could steer people down the path of love and charity, many of the problems of political philosophy would disappear. Instead, this book is filled with dry guidelines about discipline, hard work, and tolerating the Nash equilibrium bell curve of life. I do not deny that inspiration and hope are important and are largely missing from my book, unless you are inspired by philosophical arguments, but the focus of this book is the narrow path of social progress, and we cannot achieve this by decree, legislation, or platitudes. Imagine a humble factory worker who grinds away year after year to an early grave to provide a better life for his children—not inspiring or feel good, but silently heroic. I, like most people, would love to have world peace, for the fortunate to help the needy, and for the wars to end, but that is neither here nor there because the challenge is to create the wealth and social capital that would make such a dream possible. I would say, however, if you are fortunate in life and do not recognize the role of other people or society in your success, or feel you can turn a blind eye to those in need, you probably have a long journey ahead of you that will be difficult, revealing, and humbling. The great spiritual teachers always reach the same conclusion: the world is full of suffering.

As I noted in the introduction, I am not proposing that we should strive incessantly to advance along the narrow path of social progress, because there are many people, like the Amish, who are satisfied to live a simple life. The focus of this book: if we want to grow the economy, to expand education, to innovate with technology, to build large cities and interstate highways, and so on—to establish a modern state—we have to address many practical matters that will often force us to work against the grain. If people are satisfied to live a simple life in a commune, sharing everything in an egalitarian manner, then most of the ideas in this book do not apply. Go forth and conquer. However, this should be with the understanding that we are not designed to forage for berries and lounge around in the open air. We are not flip phones; we are smart phones with many fun and interesting apps that have to be activated and which allow us to rise to new levels of complexity and intellectual refinement. When Newton discovered the secrets of the universe and Mozart composed symphonies, they were living in a state of nature in the sense of living in accordance with their full potential.

As an example, consider a person with a hobby who aspires to transform it into a business. If the person is happy to continue as a hobby (doing it for fun, on his own time, perhaps even taking small loses), there is no need to get bogged down with the rigors of running a business, which for many people is probably the best option. However, if the person makes a conscious decision to transition to a profitable business, the person will have to make changes—seeking out clients and venues to sell, making products that satisfy an existing demand at a price people are willing to pay, seeking out the right suppliers, and most important, fine tuning the business model until it transforms into a positive cash flow machine. This is accomplished by fitting the mathematics of the business into accounting reports—income statement, balance sheet, and statement of cash flow. The most important part is there are tried and true ways to make this transition that do not care about our feelings or preferences. Many people strive to be true to their craft when making the transition to a business, but important decisions have to be made that often involve "compromising" or "selling out." Genre novels outsell literary novels by a wide margin. Diet books outsell philosophy books by a wide margin. The same goes for society. I would love for all people to have the luxury to pursue artistic purity and share the wealth, but if we make the conscious decision to transition to a modern state, we will collectively have to do some "compromising" and "selling out" to take care of the business that needs to be taken care of to sustain and grow the system. This is admittedly not inspirational, but the best chance we have of pursuing artistic purity or authenticity in our own lives is in a modern state, so let's make the best of it.

Second, the critic might note an unexplained inconsistency between promoting the refinement of institutional activity (less liberty) and being satisfied with Nash equilibrium in society (more liberty). The thinking goes like this: if we as a society, in the name of liberty, should be willing to accept suboptimal behavior from people within the bell curve distribution of refinement in society, why should we demand that institutions pursue perfection at the expense of personal liberty, which makes it more difficult for people from poverty or other challenging situations to work their way to the top of the social pyramid? These critics seems to believe things should work the other way: perhaps we should demand more from people in society (less liberty) and demand more from institutions in terms of accommodating individuals (more liberty), which is the opposite of what this book promotes.

Regarding society, there is a tendency by some to define liberty as doing what you want without scrutiny or judgment. The problem with this view is it has nothing to do with liberty because liberty demands that we satisfy our social obligations and accept that people are free to criticize others and associate with whomever they choose. It would be great if people were more tolerant and understanding of other people, on both sides of the political spectrum, but some attitudes and actions merit criticism, and adulthood demands that we not try to insulate ourselves from the opinions of others. After all, the dialectical process of social interaction is where we develop and refine the values we live by that will stand the test of time. Regarding institutions, there is a tendency to think institutions have an obligation to accommodate people and all their needs—pay, vacation, sick leave, health insurance, education benefits, and so on. There is no doubt people would live more satisfying lives if companies paid them more money and gave them more benefits, but of equal or more importance is whether the company would survive or whether someone else would be willing to do the job for less pay or fewer benefits. The unfortunate reality for many people is the cash flow reality of the business often will not align with their personal cash flow reality.

The best part of political philosophy is we have to make decisions about how to live, after we think and pontificate, with the understanding many people behave in ways that are not consistent with their avowed beliefs. I have no problem with people living how they want to live as long as the principle goes both ways, which is what liberty is all about. If people demand that others respect them and not criticize or pass judgment on them, then those same people must waive their right to criticize or pass judgment on others. As the evidence makes clear, however, this is not the case because there is no shortage of criticism and judgment from people on the left and the right, and I happen to be of the opinion that society benefits when people criticize and pass judgment on each other in a productive way. If you truly believe there is nothing wrong with what you believe or how you live, you should be prepared to explain why without being outraged. Regarding institutions, for the people who believe people should make more money and receive more benefits I would invite them to risk their own money to start a business, to put their money where their mouth is—to get some skin in the game. This us versus them attitude has some justification, because big businesses often make it difficult for the little guy to succeed, but as a practical matter, we all should have the intellectual integrity to understand the mathematics of life will win the day, and we will have to find a way to live that embraces some values at the expense of others.

Selected Bibliography

Abbott, H. Porter, *The Cambridge Introduction to Narrative* (Cambridge: Cambridge University Press, 2002).

Aeschylus, *The Complete Greek Tragedies*, Vol. I, edit. David Grene and Richmond Lattimore (Chicago: Chicago University Press, 1991).

Aristophanes, *Four Plays by Aristophanes*, trans. by William Arrowsmith, Richmond Lattimore, and Douglass Parker (New York: Meridian, 1994).

Aristotle, *The Complete Works of Aristotle*, Vol. 1, edit. Jonathan Barnes (Princeton, Princeton University Press, 1995).

——. *The Complete Works of Aristotle*, Vol. 2, edit. Jonathan Barnes (Princeton, Princeton University Press, 1995).

——. *The Basic Works of Aristotle*, edit. Richard McKeon (New York: Random House, 1941).

Axe, Douglas, *Undeniable: How Biology Confirms our Intuition that Life is Designed* (New York: Harper One, 2016).

Baghavad-Gita: The Song of God (New York: Signet Classic, 2002).

Bal, Mieke, *Narratology: Introduction to the Theory of Narrative* (Toronto: University of Toronto Press, 1999).

Barzini, Luigi, *The Italians: A Full-Length Portrait Featuring Their Manners and Morals* (New York: Touchstone, 1996).

Baumohl, Bernard, *The Secrets of Economic Indicators: Hidden Clues to Future Economic Trends and Investment Opportunities* (Upper Saddle Valley, NJ: Prentice River, 2008).

Becker, Ernest, *The Denial of Death* (New York: Free Press, 1973).

Bernstein, Peter L., *Against the Gods: The Remarkable Story of Risk* (New York: John Wiley & Sons, 1998).

———. *Capital Ideas: The Improbable Origins of Modern Wall Street* (New York: Free Press, 1993).

Booth, Mark, *The Secret History of the World: As Laid Down by the Secret Societies* (New York: Overlook Press, 2008).

Calasso, Roberto, *The Marriage of Cadmus and Harmony*, trans. Tim Parks (New York: Vintage, 1994).

———. *Literature and the Gods*, trans. Tim Parks (New York: Knopf, 2001).

———. *The Ruin of Kasch*, trans. William Weaver and Stephen Sartarelli (New York: Belknap Press, 1994).

Campbell, Joseph, *The Hero with a Thousand Faces* (Princeton: Princeton University Press, 1973).

Casebeer, William D., *Natural Ethical Facts: Evolution, Connectionism, and Moral Cognition* (Cambridge, MA: The MIT Press, 2003).

Cassirer, Ernst, *The Philosophy of Symbolic Forms: Language*, Vol. 1, trans. Ralph Manheim (New Haven: Yale University Press, 1955).

———. *The Philosophy of Symbolic Forms: Mythical Thought*, Vol. 2., trans. Ralph Manheim (New Haven, Yale University Press, 1955).

Castiglione, Baldesar, *The Book of the Courtier*, trans. George Bull (New York: Penguin Books, 1976).

Childers, J. J., *Asset Protection 101: Tax and Legal Strategies of the Rich* (Hoboken, NJ: John Wiley & Sons, 2008).

Coll, Steve, *Ghost Wars: The Secret History of the CIA, Afghanistan, and Bin Laden, from the Soviet Invasion to September 10, 2001* (New York: Penguin Books, 2004).

Collingwood, R. G. *The Principles of Art* (Oxford: Oxford University Press, 1958).

Copleston, Frederick. *A History of Philosophy, Vol 1: Greece and Rome From the Pre-Socratics to Plotinus* (New York: Image, 1993).

———. *A History of Philosophy, Vol. 2: Medieval Philosophy: From Augustine to Duns Scotus* (New York: Image, 1993).

———. *A History of Philosophy, Vol. 3: Late Medieval and Renaissance Philosophy: Ockhan, Francis Bacon, and the Beginning of the Modern World* (New York: Image, 1993).

———. *A History of Philosophy, Vol. 4: Modern Philosophy: From Descartes to Leibnitz* (New York: Image, 1993).

———. *A History of Philosophy, Vol. 5: Modern Philosophy: The British Philosopher from Hobbes to Hume* (New York: Image, 1993).

———. *A History of Philosophy, Vol. 6: Modern Philosophy: From the French Enlightenment to Kant* (New York: Image, 1993).

——. *A History of Philosophy, Vol. 7: Modern Philosophy: From the Post-Kantian Idealists to Marx, Kierkegaard, to Nietzsche* (New York: Image, 1994).

——. *A History of Philosophy, Vol. 8: Modern Philosophy: Empiricism, Idealism, and Pragmatism in Britain and America* (New York: Image, 1994).

——. *A History of Philosophy, Vol. 9: Modern Philosophy: From the French Revolution to Sartre, Camus, and Levi-Strauss* (New York: Image, 1994).

Cornford, F. M., *From Religion to Philosophy: A Study in the Origins of Western Speculation* (Mineola, NY: Dover Publications, 2004).

Covel, Michael W., *Trend Following: Learn to Make Millions in Up or Down Markets* (Upper Saddle River, NJ: FT Press, 2009).

Damasio, Antonio, *The Feeling of What Happens: Body and Emotion in the Making of Consciousness* (New York: Mariner Books, 2000).

Dawkins, Richard, *The Selfish Gene* (Oxford, Oxford University Press, 1990).

——. *The Blind Watchmaker: Why the Evidence of Evolution Reveals a Universe Without Design* (New York: W. W. Norton & Company, 1996).

Defoe, Daniel, *Robinson Crusoe* (New York: Bantam Books, 1982).

Dodds, E. R., *The Greeks and the Irrational* (Los Angeles, University of California Press, 1997).

——. *Pagan and Christian in an Age of Anxiety* (Cambridge: Cambridge University Press, 2001).

Dulles, Allen W., *The Craft of Intelligence* (Guilford, CT: The Lyon's Press, 2006).

Durant, Will, *The Story of Philosophy* (New York: Pocket Books, 1991).

Elder, Dr. Alexander, *Trading for a Living: Psychology, Trading Tactics, Money Management* (New York: John Wiley & Sons, 1993).

Elderman, Gerald M., *Wider than the Sky: The Phenomenal Gift of Consciousness* (New Haven, CT: Yale University Press, 2005).

Elderman, Gerald; Tononi, Giulio, *A Universe of Consciousness: How Matter Becomes Imagination* (New York: Basic Books, 2001).

Euripides, *The Complete Greek Tragedies*, Vol. III, edit. David Grene and Richmond Lattimore (Chicago: Chicago University Press, 1992).

——. *The Complete Greek Tragedies*, Vol. IV, edit. David Grene and Richmond Lattimore (Chicago: Chicago University Press, 1992).

Fauconnier, Giles; Turner, Mark, *The Way We Think: Conceptual Blending and the Mind's Hidden Complexities* (New York: Basic Books, 2003).

Ferguson, Niall, *The Ascent of Money: A Financial History of the World* (New York: Penguin Books, 2009).

——. *Civilization: The West and the Rest* (New York: Penguin Books, 2011).

Fox, Robin Lane, *Alexander the Great* (New York: Penguin Books, 1986.)

Fromkin, David, *A Peace to End All Peace: The Fall of the Ottoman Empire and the Creation of the Modern Middle East* (New York: Holt Paperback, 2001).

Ferguson, Niall, *The Ascent of Money: A Financial History of the World* (New York: Penguin Books, 2009).

Feser, Edward, *The Last Superstition: A Refutation of the New Atheism* (South Bend, IN: St. Augustine's Press, 2008).

———. *Scholastic Metaphysics: A Contemporary Introduction* (Piscataway, NJ: Transaction Books, 2014).

———. *Philosophy of Mind* (London: Oneworld Publications, 2015).

Flew, Anthony; with Varghese, Roy Abraham, *There is a God: How the World's Most Notorious Atheist Changed His Mind* (New York: Harper One, 2008).

Franklin, James, *An Aristotelian Realist Philosophy of Mathematics: Mathematics and the Science of Quantity and Structure* (New York: Palgrave Macmillan, 2014).

Fukuyama, Francis, *Political Order and Political Decay: From the Industrial Revolution to the Globalization of Democracy* (New York: Farrar, Straus and Giroux, 2014).

———. *The Origins of Political Order: From Prehuman Times to the French Revolution* (New York: Farrar, Straus and Giroux, 2010).

———. *Trust: The Social Virtues and the Creation of Prosperity* (New York: Free Press, 1996).

———. *The Great Disruption: Human Nature and the Reconstitution of Social Order* (New York: Free Press, 1999).

———. *The End of History and the Last Man* (New York: Free Press, 1992).

———. *State-Building: Governance and World Order in the 21st Century* (Ithaca, NY: Cornell University Press, 2004).

Gardner, John, *On Becoming a Novelist* (New York: W. W. Norton & Company, 1999).

George, Alexander; Velleman, Daniel J., *Philosophies of Mathematics* (Oxford: Blackwell Publishers, 2002)

Gilpin, Robert, *The Political Economy of International Relations* (Princeton, Princeton University Press, 1987).

Girard, Rene, *Deceit, Desire, and the Novel: Self and Other in Literary Structure* (Baltimore: John Hopkins Press, 1976).

———. *Things Hidden Since the Foundation of the World* (Stanford: Stanford University Press, 1987).

———. *The Scapegoat* (Baltimore: John Hopkins University Press, 1989).

——. *Violence and the Sacred* (Baltimore: John Hopkins University Press, 1979).

——. *I See Satan Fall Like Lighting* (Maryknoll, NY: Orbis Books, 2001).

Gladwell, Malcolm, *Blink: The Power of Thinking Without Thinking* (New York: Back Bay Books, 2007).

——. *Outliers: The Story of Success* (New York: Back Bay Books, 2011).

——. *Tipping Point: How Little Thinks Can Make a Big Difference* (New York: Back Bay Books, 2002).

Gracian, Baltazar, *The Art of Worldly Wisdom*, trans. Joseph Jacobs (Boston, Shambhala, 2000).

Greene, Brian, *The Elegant Universe: Superstrings, Hidden Dimensions, and the Quest for the Ultimate Theory* (New York: W. W. Norton & Company, 2003).

Greene, Robert, *Mastery* (New York: Viking, 2012).

——. *The 48 Laws of Power* (New York: Penguin Books, 1998).

Griffin, G. Edward, *The Creature from Jekyll Island: A Second Look as the Federal Reserve* (Westlake Village, CA: American Media, 2002).

Haidt, Jonathan, *The Righteous Mind: Why Good People are Divided by Politics and Religion* (New York: Vintage Publishing, 2012).

Hamilton, Edith, *The Greek Way* (New York: W. W. Norton & Company, 1993).

Hanson, Victor David; Heath, John, *Who Killed Homer?: The Demise of Classical Education and the Recovery of Greek Wisdom* (New York: Free Press, 1998).

Haqqani, Husain, *Pakistan: Between Mosque and Military* (Washington, DC: Carnegie Endowment for International Peace, 2005).

Harari, Yuval Noah, *Homo Deus: A Brief History of Tomorrow* (New York: Harper, 2017).

Havil, Julian, *The Irrationals: A Story of the Numbers You Can't Count On* (Princeton, Princeton University Press, 2012).

Hawking, Stephen, *A Brief History of Time* (New York: Bantam Books, 1998).

Hearder, Harry, *Italy: A Short History* (Cambridge: Cambridge University Press, 2007).

Heilbroner, Robert L., *The Worldly Philosophers: The Lives, Times, and Ideas of the Great Economic Thinkers* (New York: Touchstone, 1999).

Hesiod, *Theogony and Works and Days* (Oxford, Oxford University Press, 1988).

Hesse, Hermann, *Siddhartha* (New York: Bantam Classic, 1981).

Hofstadter, Douglas R., *Gödel, Escher, Bach: An Eternal Golden Braid* (New York: Basic Books, 1999).

Homer, *Iliad*, trans. Richmond Lattimore (Chicago: Chicago University Press, 1961).

———. *Odyssey*, trans. Richmond Lattimore (New York: Perennial Classics, 1999).

Hughes, James E., Jr., *Family: The Compact Among Generations* (New York: Bloomberg Press, 2007).

Hume, David, *A Treatise of Human Nature* (New York: Barnes & Noble, 2005).

Hunt, Morton, *The Story of Psychology* (New York: Anchor Books, 2007).

Huxley, Aldous, *The Perennial Philosophy*, (New York: Harper Perennial, 2009).

———. *Brave New World & Brave New World Revisited* (New York: Harper Perennial, 1965).

Innis, Robert E., *Susanne Langer in Focus: The Symbolic Mind* (Bloomington, IN: Indiana University Press, 2009).

Jaynes, Julian, *The Origin of Consciousness in the Breakdown of the Bicameral Mind* (Boston: Houghton Mifflin, 1990).

Johnson, Paul, *Modern Times: The World from the Twenties to the Eighties* (New York: Harper and Row, 1985).

Joyce, James, *A Portrait of the Artist as a Young Man* (New York: Penguin Books, 1993).

Kahneman, Daniel, *Thinking, Fast and Slow* (New York: Farrar, Straus and Giroux, 2013).

Kenny, Anthony, *A New History of Western Philosophy*, (Oxford: Oxford University Press, 2010).

Kindlon, Dan; Thompson, Michael: *Raising Cain: Protecting the Emotional Life of Boys* (New York: Ballantine Books, 2000).

Kinzer, Stephen, *All the Shah's Men: An American Coup and the Roots of Middle Eastern Terror* (Hoboken, NJ: John Wiley & Sons, 2003).

Kissinger, Henry, *World Order* (New York: Penguin Books, 2014).

Kiyosaki, Robert T., *Rich Dad's Increase Your Financial IQ: Get Smarter with Your Money* (New York: Business Plus, 2008).

Lakoff, George; Johnson, Mark, *Philosophy in the Flesh: the Embodied Mind and its Challenge to Western Thought* (New York: Basic Books, 1999).

———. *Metaphors We Live By* (Chicago: University of Chicago Press, 2003).

Langer, Susanne K., *Philosophy in a New Key: A Study in the Symbolism of Reason, Rite, and Art* (Cambridge, MA: Harvard University Press, 1979).

———. *Feeling and Form* (New York: Charles Scribner's Sons, 1953).

Le Bon, Gustave, *The Crowd: A Study of the Popular Mind* (Atlanta, Cherokee Publishing Company, 1994).

Lieven, Anatol, *Pakistan: A Hard Country* (New York: PublicAffairs, 2012).

Limbaugh, David, *Jesus on Trial: A Lawyer Affirms the Truth of the Gospel* (Washington, D.C.: Regnery Publishing, 2014).

——. *The Emmaus Code: Finding Jesus in the Old Testament* (Washington, D.C.: Regnery Publishing, 2015).

——. *The True Jesus: Uncovering the Divinity of Christ in the Gospels* (Washington, D.C.: Regnery Publishing, 2017).

Lovett, Frank. *Rawls's 'A Theory of Justice': A Reader's Guide* (New York: Bloomsbury Academic, 2011).

Machiavelli, Niccolo, *The Prince*, trans. George Bull (London: Penguin Books, 2003).

Magee, Bryan. *The Philosophy of Schopenhauer* (Oxford: Oxford University Press, 1998).

——. *Confessions of a Philosopher: A Personal Journey Through Western Philosophy from Plato to Popper* (New York: Modern Library, 1999).

Marx, Karl; Engels, Friedrich, *The Communist Manifesto* (New York: Penguin Books, 2002).

McCullough, David, *The Path Between the Seas: The Creation of the Panama Canal, 1874-1914* (New York: Simon & Schuster, 1978).

Menand, Louis, *The Metaphysical Club: A Story of Ideas in America* (New York: Farrar, Straus and Giroux, 2002).

Merzbach, Uta C.; Boyer, Carl B., *A History of Mathematics*, Third Edition (Hoboken, NJ: John Wiley & Sons, 2011).

Meyer, Stephen C., *Darwin's Doubt: The Explosive Origin of Animal Life and the Case for Intelligent Design* (New York: HarperOne, 2013).

——. *Signature in the Cell: DNA and the Evidence for Intelligent Design* (New York: HarperOne, 2009).

Modell, Arnold H., *Imagination and the Meaningful Brain* (Cambridge, MA: The MIT Press, 2006).

Murray, Gilbert, *Five Stages of Greek Religion* (Mineola, NY: Dover Publications, 2002).

Nabokov, Vladimir. *Lolita* (New York: Vintage International, 1997).

Nozick, Robert. *Anarchy, State, and Utopia* (New York: Basic Books, 2013).

Paglia, Camille, *Sexual Personae: Art and Decadence from Nefertiti to Emily Dickenson* (New York: Vintage Books, 1991).

Patton, Anthony C., *The Political Spectrum: The Rational Foundations of Liberty and Prosperity* (New York: Algora Publishing, 2015).

Pears, David. *The False Prison: A Study of the Development of Wittgenstein's Philosophy*, Vol. 1 (Oxford: Oxford University Press, 1987).

———. *The False Prison: A Study of the Development of Wittgenstein's Philosophy*, Vol. 2. (Oxford: Oxford University Press, 1988).

Peikoff, Leonard, *The DIM Hypothesis: Why the Lights of the West are Going Out* (New York: New American Library 2012).

Piaget, Jean; Inhelder, Barbel, *The Psychology of the Child* (New York: Basic Books, 1969).

Pinker, Steven, *Words and Rules: The Ingredients of Language* (New York: Perennial, 2000).

Placher, William C.; Nelson, Derek R., *A History of Christian Theology: An Introduction* (Louisville, KY: Westminister John Knox Press, 2013).

Plato, *Complete Works*, edit. John M. Cooper (Hackett, 1997).

Pons, Frank Moya, *The Dominican Republic: A National History* (Princeton: Markus Wiener Publishers, 1998).

Popper, Karl. *The Open Society & Its Enemies* (Princeton: Princeton University Press, 2013).

Prigogine, Ilya, *The End of Certainty: Time, Chaos, and the New Laws of Nature* (New York: Free Press, 1997).

Rand, Ayn, *Introduction to Objectivist Epistemology* (New York: Meridian, 1990).

———. *The Romantic Manifesto* (New York: Signet, 1975).

———. *The Virtue of Selfishness* (New York: Signet, 1964).

———. *Capitalism: The Unknown Ideal* (New York: Signet, 1986).

———. *The Voice of Reason: Essays in Objectivist Thought* (New York: Meridian, 1990).

———. *Philosophy: Who Needs It* (New York: Signet, 1984).

Rawls, John. *A Theory of Justice*, Revised Edition (Cambridge, MA: Harvard University Press, 1999).

Reid, Michael, *Forgotten Continent: The Battle for Latin America's Soul* (New Haven, CT: Yale University Press, 2007).

Ridley, Matt, *Genome: The Autobiography of a Species in 23 Chapters* (New York: Harper Perennial, 2006)

Roberts, J. M., *A Short History of the World* (Oxford: Oxford University Press, 1997).

Ross, Sir David. *Aristotle* (New York: Routledge, 2004).

Rothbard, Murray N., *A History of Money and Banking in the United States: The Colonial Era to World War II* (Auburn, AL: Ludwig Von Mises Institute, 2002).

Russell, Bertrand, *The History of Western Philosophy* (New York: Simon & Schuster, 1972).

———. *The Problems of Philosophy* (New York: Barnes & Noble, 2004).

——. *Introduction to Mathematical Philosophy* (Digireads.com Publishing, 2010).

Ryan, Alan. *On Politics: A History of Political Thought: From Herodotus to the Present* (2 Vol. Set) (New York: Liveright, 2012).

Schopenhauer, Arthur. *The World as Will and Representation*, Vol. 1, trans. E. F. J. Payne (Mineola, NY: Dover Publications, 1969).

——. *The World as Will and Representation*, Vol. 2, trans. E. F. J. Payne (Dover Publications, 1969).

——. *On the Fourfold Root of the Principle of Sufficient Reason*, trans. E. F. J. Payne (La Salle, IL: Open Court Classic, 1999).

——. *Prize Essay on the Freedom of the Will*, trans. E. F. J. Payne (Cambridge: Cambridge University Press, 1999).

——. *The World as Will and Representation*, Vol. 2, trans. by E. F. J. Payne (Mineola, NY: Dover Publications, 1966).

——. *On the Fourfold Root of the Principle of Sufficient Reason*, trans. by E. F. J. Payne (Chicago: Open Court, 1999).

——. *Prize Essay on the Freedom of the Will*, trans. E. F. J. Payne (Cambridge: Cambridge University Press, 1999).

Scruton, Roger. *Modern Philosophy: An Introduction and Survey* (New York: Penguin Books, 1996).

——. *Fools, Frauds and Firebrands: Thinkers of the New Left* (London: Bloomsbury Continuum, 2015).

——. *How to Be a Conservative* (London: Bloomsbury Continuum, 2014).

——. *The Uses of Pessimism* (Oxford: Oxford University Press, 2010).

——. *A Short History of Modern Philosophy: From Descartes to Wittgenstein* (New York, Routledge, 2002).

——. *Beauty: A Very Short Introduction* (Oxford: Oxford University Press, 2011).

——. *Kant: A Very Short Introduction* (Oxford: Oxford University Press, 2001).

——. *Spinoza: A Very Short Introduction* (Oxford: Oxford University Press, 2002).

Shapiro, Stewart, *Thinking About Mathematics: The Philosophy of Mathematics* (Oxford: Oxford University Press, 2011).

Skinner, Stephen, *Sacred Geometry: Deciphering the Code* (New York: Sterling Publishing, 2009).

Sophocles, *The Complete Greek Tragedies*, Vol. II, edit. David Grene and Richmond Lattimore (Chicago: Chicago University Press, 1991).

Talbot, Michael, *The Holographic Universe* (New York: Harper Perennial, 1992).

Taleb, Nassim Nicholas, *The Black Swan: The Impact of the Highly Improbable* (New York: Random House, 2007).

———. *Antifragile: Things that Gain from Disorder* (New York: Random House, 2012).

———. *Fooled by Randomness: The Hidden Role of Chance in Life and in the Markets* (New York: Random House, 2004).

Tarnas, Richard, *The Passion of the Western Mind: Understanding the Ideas that have Shaped Our World View* (New York: Ballantine Books, 1993).

Thomas, Even, *The Very Best Men: The Daring Early Years of the CIA* (New York: Simon and Schuster, 2006).

Turner, Mark, *The Literary Mind: The Origins of Thought and Language* (Oxford: Oxford University Press, 1998).

Wallace, David Foster, *Everything and More: A Compact History of Infinity* (New York: W. W. Norton, 2010).

Weatherford, Jack, *Genghis Khan and the Making of the Modern World* (New York: Broadway Books, 2005).

Weiner, Tim, *Legacy of Ashes: The History of the CIA* (New York: Anchor Books, 2008).

Wolin, Sheldon S., *Politics and Vision: Continuity and Innovation in Western Political Thought* (Princeton: Princeton University Press, 2016).

Wright, Lawrence, *The Looming Tower: Al-Qaeda and the Road to 9/11* (New York: Vintage, 2007).

Wright, Robert, *The Moral Animal: Why We Are, the Way We Are: The New Science of Evolutionary Psychology* (New York: Vintage, 1995).

———. *Nonzero: The Logic of Human Destiny* (New York: Pantheon Books, 2000).

Printed in the United States
By Bookmasters